Assessment in Early Childhood Education

ASSESSMENT IN EARLY CHILDHOOD EDUCATION

Edited by

GEVA M. BLENKIN *and* A. V. KELLY

P·C·P
Paul Chapman
Publishing Ltd

Paul Chapman Publishing Ltd
A SAGE Publications Company
6 Bonhill Street
London EC2A 4PU

British Library Cataloguing in Publication Data

Assessment in early childhood education.
  I. Blenkin, Geva M.   II. Kelly, A. V. (Albert Victor), 1931–
  372.1264

ISBN 1–85396–153–1

Typeset by Inforum Typesetting, Portsmouth

G H 9 8

CONTENTS

NOTES ON THE CONTRIBUTORS

With one exception, all the contributors to this book are members of the staff of the Faculty of Education at Goldsmiths' College. Four of them also contributed to an earlier publication, *Early Childhood Education*, which set out in detail the developmental approach to education in the early years which has long been established, maintained and practised there. This book seeks to extend that account into the field of pupil assessment.

Geva Blenkin's work and interests lie in the field of Curriculum Studies in general and the early years curriculum in particular. She was formerly headteacher of an infant school in the East End of London. Her major work at Goldsmiths' College is focused on the higher degree programmes in Early Childhood Education and Curriculum Studies, and on the provision of short INSET courses for early years teachers. Her current research interests include the evaluation of workplace nurseries – with Victoria Hurst. And notable among her publications are *The Primary Curriculum*, *The Primary Curriculum in Action* and *Early Childhood Education*, all published by Paul Chapman.

Eve Gregory's major area of interest is in bilingualism and she has published a number of articles in this field. Her current research is into the effects of early bilingualism on beginning reading. She has responsibility for co-ordinating language courses for initial teacher education at Goldsmiths' College and has provided a particular focus on bilingualism within these.

Victoria Hurst has a particular interest in the education of three- to five-year-olds, and in how teachers can use their understanding of young children to develop appropriate curriculum and assessment procedures. She is the specialist nursery expert in the team of early childhood tutors at Goldsmiths', and is engaged in research with Geva Blenkin in the evaluation of workplace nurseries. She is the author of *Planning for Early Learning*, published by Paul Chapman.

Clare Kelly was until recently a lecturer in Education at Goldsmiths' College. Her particular interest and expertise lie in the area of early literacy. She has worked in a variety of schools in the London Borough of Lambeth where she has been involved in research into the development of home-school links.

Vic Kelly is Dean of the Goldsmiths' Faculty of Education and Professor of Curriculum Studies. Within the field of Curriculum Studies, he has a particular interest in promoting a higher level of conceptual clarity than is evident in many current publications and pronouncements on the school curriculum. His publications include *The Curriculum: Theory and Practice* and *Knowledge and Curriculum Planning*, both published by Paul Chapman.

Margaret Lally has a particular interest in nursery education. She was formerly headteacher of a nursery school in Inner London and is currently working as an Early Years Consultant contributing to INSET courses across the country. Her publications include a number of journal articles and *The Nursery Teacher in Action*, again published by Paul Chapman.

Sue Pidgeon has been teaching in London schools for many years, and her main interests are young children's language and literacy development. Since 1986 she has been working at Goldsmiths' College, on the Primary PGCE course, with responsibility for the early years.

Marian Whitehead was until recently Head of the Department of Undergraduate Initial Teacher education at Goldsmiths' College and has also had direct responsibility for Early Childhood education courses within the BA (Ed.) degree programme. In addition to this involvement with the initial education of teachers, she makes a major contribution to the higher degree programmes in Language and Literature in Education and Early Childhood Education. Her main research interests are in the development of children's language and literacy and in narrative. She has published widely and is the author of *Language and Literacy in the Early Years*, also published by Paul Chapman.

INTRODUCTION

Assessment is an essential element in the educational process. It is essential because it is an integral part of that process. We progress educationally by acquiring a facility for assessing our own learning achievements and thus our own learning needs. The role of the teacher in this process is to assist in the acquisition of that facility. And it will be clear that such assistance is especially important in the early years of education.

Taking this as a starting point, this book sets out to do three things. First, it seeks to tease out the many complexities of the interrelationship of education and assessment. Second, it attempts to offer guidance to teachers in their search for approaches to assessment which will support their educational and curricular aims and purposes. And, third, it evaluates the likely impact of external, nationally 'standardized' assessment procedures on the experience, learning, development and education of children in the early years of schooling.

These three tasks are not the subject of separate chapters. Rather they form the central threads running through all of the chapters or, to change the metaphor, their common denominator. All the contributors, albeit tackling different and complementary briefs, display the same concern with all three issues and offer similar views on them.

Thus all stress the complementarity of assessment and educational provision, the need to ensure that the complexities of educational development are matched by correspondingly sophisticated forms of assessment, the importance of assessing the processes of educational development, and the personal nature of that development with the consequent need for assessment to be personalized.

Second, in seeking to guide teachers in their quest for appropriate forms of assessment, in addition to offering these concerns as basic principles for practice, all of the contributors also emphasize the superior merits of the assessments made by the teachers themselves and others, such as parents, who work with and thus *know* each child; the value of collaboration between these adults in the assessment process; the importance of the context in which assessment takes place; the advantages of continuous observation over 'one-off' testing; the case for holistic assessment of pupil capability; and, perhaps above all, if assessment is to be supportive of the continued process of educational development and advance, the need for it to focus on what children *can* do rather than on what they *cannot* do, to highlight their strengths rather than their weaknesses, to avoid placing them in what one chapter refers to as a 'no-win' situation, and, in fact, as Marian White-head suggests, to take advantage of the errors they make by using these as starting-points for their learning rather than regarding them as almost terminal deficiencies.

All of this, of course, implies that the kind of assessment that is properly and effectively integral to, and supportive of, the educational process is that which is formative and perhaps also, on occasion, diagnostic; summative assessment is external to that process and functions not as an aid to educational advance but merely as an attempt to 'measure' it, and is thus best seen as a political rather than an educational device.

It is this that leads to the third general theme which can be discerned running through all the contributions which follow – the conflict between the view of assessment which has just been summarized and the actualities of the National Curriculum testing programme. For it becomes quite clear not only that the baseline of that programme falls far short of the sophistication of the forms of assessment necessary to support and promote effective learning in the early years, but also that it is in fact counter-productive to that process. Its concerns are political rather than educational. It is intended primarily to act as a check on the teachers and the schools rather than to support the education of the pupils. As such, it is essentially summative, external to the context in which the learning is taking place, concerned to discover deficiencies rather than to build on strengths. Furthermore, it is less intellectually demanding than proper forms of teacher assessment, and thus may more readily be embraced by busy teachers who will recognize not only the value placed on this form of assessment by those who take it upon themselves to evaluate their effectiveness as teachers, but also the corresponding lack of respect for those more demanding forms whose justification is educational and which, politically, are to be discouraged as being not easily penetrable.

One aspect of the impact of this kind of external and decontextualized form of testing, then, which emerges from what follows is its implications for the quality of the educational experience to be offered to the children, and especially those, such as bilingual pupils, who do not come from that single-mindedly British cultural background which is the setting for the national tests.

Another aspect is its effects on the development of a proper body of professional theory for teachers, since there is no doubt that it is when teachers actively and continuously assess not only the progress of their pupils but also the impact of their own work with those pupils, and are able to translate those assessments into practical planning and provision, that they are able to develop the kinds of theoretical insights upon which good practice, at all levels of education but perhaps especially in the early years, depends.

These, then, are some of the major themes which emerge from the contributions which follow. The first two chapters aim to set the scene by exploring different concepts of, and approaches to, assessment and providing the kind of overview which creates the context for the discussions that follow. In Chapters 3 and 4, Victoria Hurst and Margaret Lally examine assessment in the nursery school, and demonstrate very clearly that the nursery school perspective, perhaps because it is there that the personal and caring nature of educational provision is most easily recognizable, offers many insights into the key features of educational assessment at all levels. In Chapters 5 and 6, Marian Whitehead and Sue Pidgeon look at good practice in the early years of education, stressing the merits of a developmental approach to the curriculum in that sector, and estimating the impact of the subject-based aspects of the National Curriculum testing programme. They also outline the advantages of proper forms of teacher assessment and suggest ways in which these can best be developed. In Chapter 7, Eve Gregory and Clare Kelly discuss the impact of the form of national testing which is planned for the early years on children whose first language is not English, and illustrate how the linguistic strengths of the bilingual pupil are not only lost but also become a handicap in this mono-lingual, and monocultural, programme. And finally, in Chapter 8, we confront directly the political face of the testing programme and consider the impact on pupils of this attempt to achieve through tests of their attainment a system of appraisal and accountability for their schools and teachers.

As we said at the beginning of this Introduction, assessment is an essential element in the educational process. To support that process, however, and to ensure that it is genuinely educational, we must have the right kind of assessment. This book sets out to show both what that kind of assessment might look like and that it bears little resemblance to the public forms of testing which are currently being implemented for our schools.

1
CONCEPTS OF ASSESSMENT: AN OVERVIEW

Vic Kelly

It seems to be unfashionable these days, especially in education, to engage in conceptual clarification, to seek out carefully the precise meanings of words. To do so is seen as 'theorizing' and often this is contrasted unfavourably with 'getting on with things', with the practice of education. Yet there can be no practice without theory; and there can be no sound practice without sound theory; and so not to get one's meanings clarified is to risk diminishing the quality of one's practice.

Nevertheless, many of the statements about education which one sees issuing from a number of sources, including those instructing and advising us on official policy, use subtle and problematic terms as though they were straightforward and uncomplicated, terms which may bear many different meanings and nuances of meaning as though they have only one, obvious, common meaning, familiar to all who use them. One such term is 'education' itself; another is 'curriculum'; a third is 'assessment'.

Assessment has been a central concern in the educational debate and in practice throughout the 1980s, a period which has been described as 'the era of assessment-led educational reform' (Hargreaves, 1989, p. 99), and during which 'assessment, more than curriculum or pedagogy' has been 'the prime focal point for educational change' (ibid.). Evidence of this is mainly to be found, of course, in changes which have occurred in the secondary sector of schooling, the advent of the GCSE, for example, the development of schemes of graded assessment and the arrival of the Certificate of Prevocational Education (CPVE). And it may thus be seen as reflecting that increased emphasis on vocational aspects of schooling, on preparation for 'the world of work', on ensuring that pupils are equipped with 'the knowledge, skills and understanding that they need for adult life and employment' (DES, 1987a, p. 3). These influences, however, have extended into the primary school, and even into nursery and first schools. The development of such schemes as the late Inner London Education Authority's Primary Language Record provides one piece of evidence that assessment has become a major concern in this sector, and it is certainly the case that the generation of industrial awareness in pupils has been in recent years pressed as much on teachers of young children as on those concerned with the final years of schooling.

The arrival of the National Curriculum has sharpened this focus on assessment at all levels, since it is now a legal requirement that children be tested at the four 'key stages', 7+, 11+, 14+ and 16+. It has also led to a hardening of the view taken of the role of assessment in education, a shift from that developing concern at all levels with profiling and personal records of achievement to an emphasis on standardized testing of a kind that is expected to provide evidence of success (and thus also of failure) to all those who are regarded as the 'consumers' of educational provision. And, whether this assessment is statutory or non-statutory, it is being pressed upon schools and teachers at all levels as the focal point of their professional concerns.

It is perhaps worth stressing here the impact of this accelerated move towards increased external testing even where such testing is non-statutory, not least because of the significance of this for those working in the nursery or pre-school sector. For, first of all, there is the inevitable 'top-down' or 'backlash' effect of statutory testing at key stage 1, at 7+. Indeed, this has already reached the point where some people are suggesting that pupils need to be tested on entry to statutory schooling at age five, or rising-five, in order that we may have a yardstick against which to measure their progress when we test them formally at 7+. Results of testing at 7+, it is argued, will be of little significance – especially as a device for evaluating the competence of the school and its teachers – unless we know where each child started from. (The logic of this is interesting since it must ultimately lead to testing at the very moment of birth!)

We should note too that all teacher training, including that of intending nursery teachers, is directly linked to the National Curriculum and thus to its testing programme. Further, attempts are being made currently not only to assess intending nursery teachers against the same criteria as are applied to other teachers in training (especially in respect of their knowledge of an approved curriculum 'subject'), but also to develop 'performance indicators' which can be used to assess and certificate all professionals working with the under-sevens.

We must be very clear, then, from the outset that, whether it is statutory or non-statutory, external testing is not something which can be ignored by teachers working at any level or in any sector of the education service and, because of the particular unsuitability of public forms of assessment in the education of very young children, especially those working with children in the early years. For the main focus of current educational policy is on external testing, reflecting that emphasis we noted earlier, as is plain from the fact that the first stage in the development of that policy was the work of the Task Group on Assessment and Testing (TGAT) (DES, 1988a), and that has serious implications for all sectors, including that of the nursery school.

It is thus important that we begin our discussion of the implications of this shift for the education of children in the early years with an attempt to identify the different meanings the term 'assessment' may have, the ways in which those meanings will, or may, relate to the different contexts in which it is being used at any one time, and the different implications and effects those meanings will have for our educational practice.

This chapter, therefore, sets out to prepare the ground for the more specific discussions which later chapters will undertake. It will do this, first, by drawing attention to the multifaceted nature of the concept of assessment, the many different purposes it may have and, indeed, its many different effects. In short, we will begin by attempting to identify some of the features which make this a highly problematic concept. Next, we will highlight the integral relationship between assessment and the curriculum, and especially between different forms or modes or views of assessment and different concepts of curriculum. For, although we are constantly being told these days that assessment 'should be the servant, not the master, of the curriculum' (DES, 1988d, para. 4; DES, 1989a), there is little evidence that any attempt has been made to acknowledge, let alone to act upon, the subtleties of the interrelationships between assessment procedures and curricular practices, and there is every indication that we are moving to a curriculum which is in every sense assessment-led or, worse, test-led.

This, of course, has particular significance for the curriculum in the early years, which, having traditionally been free of the constraints of public forms of assessment, has developed differently from (and, some would say, a good deal further than) the curriculum at other levels of educational provision. We will note, therefore, its particular impact there, since this will form the substance of what the following chapters will seek to explore in greater detail.

Finally, since it seems that the current preoccupation with external testing is directed more at establishing means for controlling the curriculum than at raising the educational quality of what is offered to pupils in school, whatever the rhetoric with which it is presented, we will consider briefly the relationship between assessment and control, especially as this is revealed by a cursory survey of the development of systems of public assessment in the United Kingdom.

THE CONCEPT OF EDUCATIONAL MEASUREMENT

Assessment is often spoken of as educational measurement, and it is worth beginning our discussion by considering briefly this notion of measuring educational progress or attainment. The term 'measurement' brings with it connotations of precision and accuracy. Yet, when we look into matters more closely we are forced to recognize that there is little that is precise or accurate about most forms of assessment in education, and thus to acknowledge that it can seldom, if ever, be regarded as measurement in any mathematical sense of the term. Only if we are attempting to assess the most unsophisticated forms of achievement can we be sure of reaching any reasonable level of accuracy, and even then 100 per cent accuracy will be unlikely.

For, if we wish to discover how many pupils know that $2 \times 3 = 6$, we can set a test item, $2 \times 3 = ?$, and establish with some accuracy and precision which of them, and what proportion of them, can give us the right answer, although even here we cannot easily allow for carelessness, lack of motivation or interest or understanding of the question, or any other factor which might affect pupil performance and thus the accuracy of our 'measurement'. If we wish, however, to discover whether they *understand* that $2 \times 3 = 6$, and/or *why* this is so, even the most sophisticated test instrument we can devise will not give us anything like the same level of accuracy. And if, further, we wish to discover whether there is behind this performance any understanding of the concept of multiplication, the level of accuracy we can hope for will be even lower, and so on. Accuracy of assessment is related inversely to the complexity and the sophistication of what is being assessed. And, since education is a highly complex and sophisticated process, educational assessment can be regarded as measurement only in the remotest of metaphorical senses.

So, whenever and wherever it has been regarded as more reliable than this, and especially when and where the data gleaned from assessment exercises have been used as a basis for prediction, for the making of far-reaching decisions about educational provision, such decisions have been fraught with inaccuracies and thus with errors. The use of 11+ testing to allocate pupils to supposedly suitable forms of secondary education is probably the most notable, and infamous, example of this; but one also notes the low levels of correlation between GCE O- and A-level grades, and, especially, between A-level grades and degree classifications among those pupils who go on to universities or polytechnics. Accuracy of measurement is assumed, and that assumption is even acted upon, but all the evidence is that it is a myth, a chimera, an attractive but totally fanciful conception.

Educational assessment, therefore, must be recognized as being a highly imprecise activity at all but the most basic of levels, and as being judgemental rather than metric in character, as requiring the making of sound professional judgements rather than of objective, mathematical measurements. Nor is this only because, in spite of every effort, no one has yet come up with a scheme of assessment or a set of test instruments that are capable of yielding accurate data. The TGAT report (DES, 1988a) has drawn our attention to the fact that 'no system has yet been constructed that meets all the criteria of *progression, moderation, formative* and *criterion-referenced* assessment' (op. cit., para. 13), and it goes on to say 'Our task has therefore been to devise such a system afresh' (ibid.). Even if one does not raise the question of the morality of instituting by law an elaborate assessment system which is as untried, as experimental and as unformed as those quotations would suggest, one can ask whether the non-existence of such a system is a result of previous lack of ingenuity, as would seem to be implied, or of a much more fundamental conceptual difficulty which would not only explain why such a system has not yet been devised but would also imply the impossibility of our ever devising it.

It might further be argued that this very problem of accuracy, or rather the overwhelming evidence of the inevitable inaccuracies of testing of this kind, should draw our attention not to continued attempts at squaring the circle but towards a search for some kind of alternative form of assessment, and to a deeper exploration of the role of assessment in education (Broadfoot, 1986).

For one of the reasons why accurate measurement of educational attainment has proved impossible is that education, however one conceives it, is a highly personal matter since it involves human beings, every one of whom has his/her own characteristics. It is for this reason that any attempts to standardize what we mean by educational attainment must lead to a diminution of our notion of what it is to be seen to consist of, a reduction to its lowest common denominator; and this is also why to use our 'measurements' of attainment against that LCM as predictors of future personal performance must lead to inaccuracies of the kind we have just noted. If one accepts, then, that education is a personal matter – and, even if one does not accept that as an educational ideology, it is difficult to deny the empirical evidence that it is in truth the practical outcome of all our attempts to educate, no matter how standardized – then one must see the attempt to standardize our definition of education (through common attainment targets, profile components, programmes of study and the rest) and our forms of assessment (into the same categories) as a process that must inevitably remove that personal dimension from it, and thus take away what is the essence not only of the concept of education to which many people subscribe, but also of the reality of the educational experience for all.

The concept of educational measurement, then, represents not only a denial of those educational ideologies which have at their root the notion of the uniqueness of every human being, but also of the realities of the practice of education, which manifestly results in personalized forms of curriculum being 'received' by every child. For it acknowledges individual differences, as psychometric versions of educational psychology do, at the level only of differences in rates of progress along predetermined routes and not in terms of the many facets of the uniqueness of each pupil and his/her response to the educational experiences he/she is offered. It is for this reason that the terms 'personal' and 'personalized' are used here, to stress a view of the uniqueness of individual experience which embraces far more than rates, or even styles, of learning.

What is needed to acknowledge that personal dimension is a recognition that assessment is of personal experience and not merely of individual progress, that it is a matter of judgement rather than of measurement, and that, as a consequence, the standards against which such judgements can best be made are those based on the characteristics and previous achievement of each pupil rather than on those of his/her peers or those derived from some external and impersonal concept or definition either of particular subjects or of the educational process itself. This provides at least a *prima facie* case for ipsative forms of assessment rather than those which are either criterion-referenced or norm-referenced. It also begins to raise other issues about forms of assessment and their implications for the curriculum. It thus takes us naturally on to our next major section.

FORMS OF ASSESSMENT

The TGAT Report (DES, 1988a, para. 23) lists for us several purposes that the data produced by the National Curriculum assessment programme should be capable of fulfilling:

- *formative*, so that the positive achievements of a pupil may be recognised and discussed and the appropriate next steps may be planned;
- *diagnostic*, through which learning difficulties may be scrutinised and classified so that appropriate remedial help and guidance can be provided;
- *summative*, for the recording of the overall achievement of a pupil in a systematic way;
- *evaluative*, by means of which some aspects of the work of a school, an LEA or other discrete part of the educational service can be assessed and/ or reported upon.

Although the report itself recommends that assessment should be *summative* at key stage 4 (16+) only, a subsequent DES publication (DES, 1989b) has indicated that it is to be summative at all stages, indeed at every stage it is to be formative, summative, evaluative, informative and 'helpful for professional development' (op. cit., para. 6.2). Apart from asking whether any one system could ever be devised that would attain all of these different purposes at the same time, and noting that the implementation of the scheme as reflected in the DES document has already jettisoned some of the niceties (and thus some of the safeguards) of the TGAT Report, we need to dwell for a moment on the significance of these distinctions.

We will leave aside for the moment those purposes which relate more to the professional development of teachers and/or the evaluation of the local authority, the school or even the curriculum, and concentrate on those aspects of this analysis which relate to pupil assessment or the assessment of pupil performance. If we do so, two distinctions emerge which require further attention. The first of these is that between the *formative* and the *diagnostic* functions of assessment; the second that between the *formative* and the *diagnostic* taken together and the *summative*.

Formative and diagnostic assessment

The TGAT Report itself indicated that it did not see the boundary between these two forms or purposes of assessment 'as being sharp or clear' (op. cit., para. 27) and recommended 'that the basis of the national assessment system be essentially formative, but designed also to indicate where there is need for more detailed diagnostic assessment' (ibid.).

A clear distinction should perhaps be drawn, however, between the positive and the negative dimensions of these aspects of assessment. The connotations of the term 'formative', indeed the definition of it offered by the TGAT Report, would suggest that its function is the largely positive one of taking the pupil's education forward – presumably to something further and better. Diagnostic assessment, on the other hand, again as the TGAT definition as well as the etymology indicates, offers the negative connotation of identifying learning difficulties, of attempting to discover where things have gone or are going wrong, in order to offer 'appropriate remedial help' (op. cit., para. 23). In short, it comes into play only when things are going wrong.

Now both of these are important functions of assessment. It is crucial, however, to recognize that they are two sides of a coin and, especially, that assessment must fulfil the positive function of helping us to decide how to assist a child to move forward as well as and, indeed, more importantly than, the negative role of enabling us to identify learning difficulties or barriers.

Another way of looking at this is to stress that formative assessment is essentially concerned to identify what a pupil *can* do, while diagnostic assessment focuses on what he/she *cannot* do. The merits of the former approach to supporting educational development are well known to most teachers and other professionals, especially those experienced at working with children in the early years, and perhaps even more so to those who work with the under-fives. They also have the 'scientific' support of those many psychological studies which have endorsed the advantages of 'positive reinforcement' over 'negative reinforcement'. Thus there is a boundary between these two forms of assessment which is conceptually both sharp and clear, and which should perhaps be kept sharp and clear at the level of practice too.

We should further note that, although we always need to identify learning difficulties a child may be experiencing, this form of diagnosis will be more appropriate, and will loom rather larger, in the context of a curriculum conceived as a predetermined body of knowledge to be assimilated by every child or objectives to be attained by everyone, than in the freer and more flexible environment of the kind of personalized provision we referred to earlier.

It is also important to note that assessment which is directed towards helping a child on, whether by identifying positive achievements or by noting learning difficulties, is the kind of assessment which, although not always formalized and perhaps not always recorded, those teachers and others who are working with children in the early years are engaged in all the time. It almost certainly follows from this that it is a form of assessment best dealt with through continuous assessment by those working with the pupil, and perhaps not achieved very effectively by the use of standardized tests or attainment tasks. For such tests or tasks are essentially *summative* in their effects, even if not in their intention. And that takes us on to a brief examination of the *summative/formative* distinction.

Summative and formative assessment

The first question to be asked in respect of this distinction is whether it is possible to maintain it in the context of standardized national assessment. One can certainly do so at the theoretical level, as the TGAT Report (DES, 1988a) has demonstrated. At the practical level, however, as the implementation of the recommendations of that report seem to have indicated, it is much more difficult, if not impossible, to maintain. Standardized tests must always be summative. They cannot, as the TGAT Report proposed, be formative and/or diagnostic only. A summative effect is inevitable, even if it is not intended, and cannot be delayed until 16+, even if it were the accepted official policy that it should be so. One notes in this connection the report's comment (DES, 1988a, para. 24) that 'it would be impossible to keep the burdens on teachers and pupils within reasonable bounds if different batteries of assessments and tests had to be created to serve each separate purpose' and, further, 'we must therefore reflect the priority given in our brief to the need "to show what a pupil has learned and mastered" ' (ibid.). In short, even within the TGAT Report itself, summative assessment is supreme at all key stages.

The real issue is whether standardized tests can be formative and/or diagnostic at the same time as being summative. Every indication points to the conclusion that it may be impossible to satisfy these disparate require-ments through the same forms of assessment, not least since, as we have just suggested, the formative requirement is not most easily and effectively met through standardized tests, while standardized tests of some kind are essential if we are to achieve the summative purpose of recording 'the overall achievement of a pupil in a systematic way' (op. cit., para. 23). Hence it may be the case that, in order to achieve summative 'scores' for all pupils at the four key stages, we may have to forget about useful formative and/or diagnostic data. We probably cannot have our cake and eat it here. If our main focus is on summative assessment, then the assessment data are unlikely to offer much help of a formative or diagnostic kind. And, if we are trying to obtain diagnostic or formative data by way of standardized tests, we will not be able to free ourselves of the summative dimension of those tests.

The upshot of this would seem to be that standardized tests whose

justification is to be found mainly in the need to provide summative conclusions about a pupil's progress, to be *'informative*, in helping communication
with parents about how their child is doing; and with governing bodies,
LEAs and the wider community about the achievement of the school'
(DES, 1989b, para. 6.2) are likely to offer teachers and other professionals
working with them little that will help them to plan their further work or
that of their pupils, except within the context of rather simple learning
tasks. Another way of expressing this and, indeed, another aspect of this
policy, is that if assessment is to be undertaken primarily with administrative concerns in mind (as was the case with the old 11+) it must be *summative* at the expense of both its formative and its diagnostic dimensions. It
must concentrate on providing information for those who, albeit interested
parties, are outside the educational process itself, at the cost of offering
adequate guidance for those inside it, teachers, other professionals working
with them and the pupils themselves. Indeed, the very fact that assessment
and curriculum have been separated from each other, by the creation of
separate bodies – National Curriculum Council (NCC) and School Examination and Assessment Council (SEAC) – with responsibility for each, is
the clearest evidence we have that the main thrust of testing is summative,
since the integral, formative relationship between curriculum and assessment has thus been denied. If teachers and others are to continue, therefore, to make evaluations of their work with their pupils, both individually
and collectively, with a view to improving it, they will need to continue, if
they have the time, with something like their present practices and procedures, since they are likely to gain little of value in this respect from the
data which will emerge from standardized tests.

The main focus of such tests, as we have just seen, must be on their
summative function, and there are two aspects of this we must note here.
First, standardized tests of this kind, conducted on a national scale, require
the production of something upon which assessment can be based, a 'script'
of some kind which an external examiner or moderator can peruse and
assess. The production of such a 'script' by a three- or four-year-old is
difficult to envisage. If the main focus of the assessment programme is on
this kind of assessment, therefore, it is unlikely that children of this age can
be included in it. Second, the summative function of these tests can be
defined only in relation to fixed, agreed and common notions of what all
pupils must be exposed to and must learn. And that takes us naturally on to
a consideration of a further set of distinctions we need to be aware of – the
differing and contrasting implications of norm-referenced, criterion-
referenced and ipsative assessment.

Norm-referenced, criterion-referenced and ipsative assessment

Much has been made recently of the distinction between norm-referenced and criterion-referenced assessment, and again the TGAT Report (DES, 1988a) has declared its position – and thus that of the National Curriculum assessment programme – very clearly. That programme is to be criterion-referenced.

The view has been expressed, however, that this distinction is largely academic (in the sense of being theoretical rather than of being intellectually sound), since criteria tend to be determined by reference to what it is felt is, or should be the norm, and norms tend to be fixed by reference to predetermined criteria. It is difficult, if not impossible, to compare a particular child's performance with that of his/her peers without reference to some criteria of achievement; and, conversely, it is difficult to identify criteria of achievement without some reference to what is regarded as average or normal capability. One cannot assess, or at any rate one cannot assess *summatively*, the understanding a five-year-old may display of quantum theory, for example, except against some criteria derived from a concept of what it means to understand quantum theory. But, at the same time, the significance of what that child understands in this field can be judged only by reference to other children. Thus, while the attainment targets of each subject within the National Curriculum have been decided by reference to that subject and its profile components, as these have been defined in statutory orders, and are thus criterion-referenced, the levels of attainment have been determined in relation to some notion of what can reasonably be expected of pupils at given ages, and are thus norm-referenced. Assessment, however, must take account of both, so that the distinction is difficult, indeed impossible, to maintain – certainly in practice – in spite of the fact that so much has been, and is being, made of it.

Politically, of course, it is imprudent to acknowledge that the national system of testing is norm-referenced. To do so is to concede that it is competitive and thus élitist, that at least one of its functions is to attempt to measure the performance of pupil against pupil and to act as a device for identifying and selecting the most 'able'. Whether this function is acknowledged or not, however, in any form of summative assessment it must be present, and to pretend that it need not be, or is not, present is at best misguided and at worst fundamentally dishonest.

Perhaps a far more important and useful distinction, therefore, is that between both of these forms of assessment and that form which has come to be known as *ipsative* assessment. Ipsative assessment is assessment of a pupil not against norms (based on the performance of his/her peers) or against criteria (derived from particular conceptions of subjects and/or of education) but against his/her own previous levels of attainment and performance. In short, it is linked to a view of education as individual development. It has also been argued (Nuttall, 1989, p. 55) that 'the very notion of progress through levels implies an ipsative framework as much as it does a criterion-referenced one'. This may well be true. What may be more important, however, is that again we are looking at a form of assessment which, first, is much akin to what teachers and others regularly do in their classrooms by way of monitoring the progress of each child, which, second, suggests that there must be an important role for teacher assessment in the new procedures, and which, third, may reinforce the view we expressed earlier that this kind of function may not be best fulfilled by standardized forms of external testing. In short, it must be questioned whether ipsative assessment can be accomplished by the application of externally devised test instruments, however sophisticated those instruments may be.

Aggregated and holistic assessment

A final point that must be made about attempts to establish a criterion-referenced assessment scheme, and certainly that particular version of such a scheme which is currently being devised for schools in the United Kingdom, is that the criteria which are selected are derived, as was suggested earlier, from particular conceptions of the individual subjects to be examined. Thus the establishment of levels of attainment within each subject has been accompanied by attempts at definitions of what constitutes the essence of each subject, definitions focused on attainment targets, and profile components; and programmes of study have been devised, according to the terms of reference given to the subject Working Groups, to describe 'the essential content which needs to be covered to enable pupils to reach or surpass the attainment targets'.

Such a system, of course, implies a subject-based curriculum and, further, a curriculum consisting of subjects defined as seemed appropriate in 1989/90, ossified and preserved in that form and protected from the kind of continuous development which we have seen occurring over the last few decades and which we are now aware the organization of human knowledge must, for a variety of reasons, be open to. What is more important in the context of our present discussion, however, is that it also demands that the definition of each subject should be achieved by breaking it down into what are seen as its component parts. And that in turn means the assessment of pupils across each of these component parts. Assessment is thus across a range of subjects and a range of attainment targets within those subjects; and it consists of the creation of a picture of each pupil's performance, both within and between those subjects, by some form of *aggregation*.

The corollary of this, of course, is that such forms of assessment will not, and cannot, assess *holistic* capability either within subjects or in a cross-curricular form. Nor do the proposals of the TGAT Report (DES, 1988a) for the Standard Assessment Tasks (SATs) at 7+ and 11+ to 'cover a range of profile components' (op. cit., para. 153) do much to allay this concern. For we are told that the 'three or four standard tasks which cover a range of profile components', which the report recommends, should perhaps 'focus respectively on mathematical and scientific learning; on literacy and the humanities; and on aesthetics' (ibid.). So there continues to be a separation of elements (perhaps most notably the separation of literacy and the humanities from aesthetics); and, further, it is clear that, even if the SATs themselves sought to, and were cleverly devised to, cover the whole range, the assessment process, the analysis of the data they produce, must take the form of assessing pupil performance in relation to the quite separate attainment targets in the areas so covered and aggregating the results of these tests. The assessment process itself, therefore, cannot be holistic, even if the tasks attempt to be, and must consist of some kind of aggregation of scores.

We must express some concern again, therefore, at the educational implications of this kind of scheme. It is quite apparent that *educational* attainment is very much more than the sum of its parts, whether we are defining it narrowly within any one subject or area of the curriculum, or in rather broader terms. We will not be able to assess with any degree of accuracy a child's mathematical understanding merely by aggregating scores on tests of 'number, algebra and measures' with those of 'shape and space and handling data' with those of 'practical applications of mathematics'. Competence in mathematics must be recognized as a holistic capability and, if it is to be assessed, it must be assessed as such. Analysis of pupil performance in particular aspects of a subject or area of understanding is important – not least for those formative and diagnostic purposes we discussed earlier. It can be successfully achieved, however, only by a breaking down of the *performance*, not of the subject itself. In order to get a picture of a pupil's total performance, you do not assess discrete component parts and aggregate them; you try to obtain the whole picture and then analyse that into its component elements. There is every educational advantage, and justification, in seeking to assess individual pupils holistically first and then developing from that total picture an individual profile which will not only indicate the level of their performance but also, and more importantly, describe and offer an analysis of the nature of that performance, highlighting points of strength and of weakness. In educational terms, the picture that process produces is much more valuable to all concerned – parents, teachers, associated professionals and the pupils themselves. In the long run it may also be of more value to potential employers. And there is a real chance that it may satisfy any summative demands we may wish to place on it as well as its manifest contribution to formative and diagnostic assessment.

The merits of this approach, and indeed its practicality, have been clearly demonstrated by the work of the Assessment of Performance Unit's Design and Technology team, which, having adopted a definition of design and technology as a holistic capability, and, having thus declared that 'it would be inappropriate to build a monitoring programme around isolated tests of conceptual knowledge or practical skills' (DES, 1987b, p. 21), proceeded to develop tests which could first be assessed holistically – by impression marking – and then analysed, both descriptively and evaluatively, to achieve a unique picture of each pupil assessed in terms of both the nature and the level of his/her performance, its strengths and its weaknesses. The testing undertaken by this team was of course, in the context of an APU survey, anonymous. It has revealed, however, some of the enormous possibilities and potential of this form of assessment.

The case for this approach to assessment is made compellingly in an early draft of the report of that team (SEAC/EMU 1991).

> We know there are different ways of performing well in design and technology [or any other area of the curriculum or dimension of experience] and the holistic scores allowed markers to record this interactive quality without separating out and totalling the components. This allows us to look for the relationships between holism and the individual components – not in order to identify some magical combination that would provide the prescription for all good future performance, but to illustrate the variety of approaches from different groups of pupils [or individual pupils] and to diagnose particular strengths and weaknesses in approach that gives insight into ways of supporting pupils and promoting the development of capability.

In other words, there are many ways of skinning any cat, and that wide variation in the personal interpretation and performance by pupils must be recognized and catered for in any scheme of assessment which aims to be fair to all and is not predicated on the view that there is only one 'right way'.

The advantages of this kind of approach have also been recognized in, and indeed revealed by, numerous attempts to develop systems of profiling and records of achievement. The Primary Language Record, developed by the late Inner London Education Authority, is one example of such a scheme. There has also been a number of profiling systems produced for use in secondary schools. Indeed, we were promised that a national system of Records of Achievement would be in place by 1990, although this promise has subsequently been withdrawn, ostensibly because of the work that is having to be put into establishing the National Curriculum and its testing programme, but more probably because its conceptual base clashes with that of that programme.

Profiling systems or records of achievement depend to a great extent on ipsative assessment and on teacher assessment; they can be less easily adapted to externally imposed, criterion-referenced, standardized assessment tasks. They seek to be holistic and to describe all aspects of a pupil's achievement, and so they cannot be obtained merely by the aggregation of discrete collections of grades. They attempt to be formative as well as, ultimately, summative, so they must strive to maintain a focus on the personal progress of each pupil. And 'in principle, at least [they] take a rather more dynamic stance' (Torrance, 1989, p. 187) than graded tests which 'are clearly tailored to a mechanistic, if not static, view of learning' (ibid.); and so they necessitate a more open and evolutionary view of subjects, of knowledge and of curriculum than the National Curriculum permits. Finally, they acknowledge that educational assessment is a matter of judgement rather than measurement and so they do not seek to offer grades of attainment but rather to provide descriptions of and comments on performance.

Thus, we note again that doubts arise over whether any externally imposed scheme of assessment, unless very heavily tempered by teacher assessment, and that undertaken by other professionals working with teachers, and thus consisting of little more than a broad framework for such assessment, can be both summative and formative at the same time or can meet the educational needs of assessment as well as the administrative demands on it. The choice of a 'graded test' system of assessment for the National Curriculum, rather than the development of profiling or records of achievement, would seem to reinforce the view not only that that curriculum is assessment-led but also that it is so because of a prime concern with the administrative and controlling role of assessment – the sorting and grading of pupils and the appraisal of schools and teachers – rather than with its educational functions, what it might do to help pupils, and teachers too, to raise their own standards, to improve the quality of their work and to maintain the maximum level of progress on all educational fronts.

This takes us on to a consideration of some aspects of the interrelationship between assessment and the curriculum, and it is to an exploration of these that we now turn.

MODES OF ASSESSMENT AND CONCEPTS OF CURRICULUM

It was asserted earlier in this chapter that the National Curriculum is assessment-led. That it is so will have become apparent from what has been said since then, for it will be clear that the starting-point for the framing of that curriculum has been the attainment targets set for assessment. That it is assessment-led, however, is not the most significant point, although it is of course a serious matter. What is much more important is the direction in which assessment is leading the curriculum. There is nothing inherently unsatisfactory in a form of assessment which 'leads' our curriculum; everything depends on the form of that assessment, on the kind of curriculum it leads to and especially on the match or mismatch of the two.

The interrelationship of assessment and curriculum is a highly complex and sophisticated matter. First, in order to ensure the effectiveness of either, there has to be a constant interplay between them. All forms of assessment, except those of the most simplistic and unsophisticated kind, provide us with insights into, and understandings of, not only the achievements of individual pupils but also such things as the value of the curricular experiences we are offering and our effectiveness in presenting them to our pupils. And, unless we are totally insensitive, they also provide us with a critical basis from which to evaluate our assessment procedures themselves. There is thus not only scope for, but also a positive need for, a constant and regular 'feed-back' and 'feed-forward', as our curriculum is modified in the light of assessment data and our assessment procedures are themselves adapted and adjusted in the light of experience of their effects and their application. This happens even at the level of formal, external, summative assessments. It happens most notably, however, and most significantly, at the level of the formative and diagnostic assessments individual teachers, and those working with them, are continuously making of individual pupils.

This interplay between curriculum and assessment is crucial for the quality of both, and scope for such interplay to be maximized is essential for the continued development of both. It is thus disappointing, to say the least, that the two functions have been separated as decisively as they have been in the machinery which has been set up to support the implementation of the National Curriculum and its assessment programme. For to have a National Curriculum Council attending to the establishment and the maintenance of the National Curriculum from York (or from Cardiff) and a School Examinations and Assessment Council overseeing the assessment of that curriculum from Notting Hill Gate is to proclaim and enforce a distinction between the two which is belied by the experience of every teacher and which will ensure, whether this is the intention or not, that the 'feed-back/feed-forward' interplay we have just identified is not only not supported and promoted but is even inhibited. Teachers, along with those working with them, will of course continue to attempt to interrelate the two but, here again, the structures which have been created, and within which they must work, are of a kind to make their task more difficult rather than to support them, and to lead to a reduction rather than an improvement in the educational quality of their work. Such structures may well achieve an improvement in the efficiency with which they 'deliver' the curriculum planned in York (or Cardiff) by ensuring a rigidity in the assessment procedures stage-managed from Notting Hill Gate, and this may well be the intention, and the limited ambition, of those structures. If we are right, however, to claim that the quality of educational experience and the effectiveness of educational assessment depend on there being a constant and effective interplay between the two, and if, in particular, we are right to claim that such quality is a function of the continuous development of both which that interplay makes possible and promotes, then we must recognize that that quality must be diminished by a mechanism which deliberately inhibits such interplay and such development.

Secondly, we must note that this interplay goes well beyond issues of mere content, and that when we describe a curriculum, such as the National Curriculum, as 'assessment-led', we are not merely drawing attention to the fact that the assessment procedures determine the content of the curriculum. Assessment can determine not only the content of our curriculum – by setting out examination syllabuses, for example, or lists of attainment targets – it can also determine the nature of our curriculum, indeed the very concept of curriculum which we adopt and base our work as teachers upon.

Teachers and educationists generally have been aware for some time that curricula differ from one another in more subtle ways than merely through their subject-content. It has become clear, through both theoretical debate and practical curriculum planning during the last two or three decades, that there are and can be very important differences in the way in which the curriculum is conceived.

It is not the intention here to retread that ground, to explore in detail what must be more than familiar to anyone who has even the slightest acquaintance with the curriculum debate of recent years, or to elaborate on what would now have achieved the status of cliché, if it had not been so manifestly ignored in all official publications on the school curriculum, namely that the curriculum can be conceptualized and planned in terms of its content, its 'aims and objectives' or its processes.

It is important to stress here that just as the curriculum can be conceived in these three quite different ways, so can assessment; and just as these different conceptions of curriculum will lead to different curricular practice, so will different conceptions of assessment lead to different forms of assessment and of test instruments, according to whether our concern is to assess knowledge-content absorbed, aims and objectives attained, or educational processes promoted. It will be further apparent that when the assessment procedures play such a dominant part in education that they 'lead' the curriculum, they will lead it down their own paths. It thus becomes crucial that concepts of assessment, and thus forms of assessment instruments, be matched to concepts of the curricula they are designed to assess. If there is mismatch, this will lead to distortion – both of the curriculum and of the assessment data.

It will be clear, then, that the relationship between assessment and the curriculum goes well beyond questions of curriculum-content. It is because content, and content within clear subject boundaries, has for many years been the dominant feature of public assessment at 16+ that the secondary school curriculum has taken the subject-based, content-based form it has in most places. And, conversely, as was suggested earlier, it is because there has hitherto been no public assessment of pupils in first schools that the curriculum at that level has developed differently – not merely in respect of its content but in its very nature and conception.

It follows from this, therefore, that, if the National Curriculum is assessment-led, then this will lead to a form of curriculum which will match the form of assessment which has been adopted. And since, as we have seen, that form of assessment is clearly based on graded assessment objectives, on predetermined bodies of subject-content, expressed as 'aims and objectives', and since 'attainment targets are based on the objectives model of education' (Nuttall, 1989, p. 53), such a form of assessment will either lead to the adoption of that form of curriculum or it will create distortion if applied to a different form, not to mention the fact that, if so applied, it will be unlikely to produce results of any accuracy or worth. And so, if we conceive of our curriculum as process-based (Stenhouse, 1975) or as developmental (Blenkin and Kelly, 1987(a) and (b)), the form of assessment we are now facing will not match such a curriculum nor, as a result, will it assist or promote its continued development. On the contrary, it must lead to distortion, as we attempt to adapt the one to the other, when, if we are right in what we are claiming, they are incompatible – both conceptually and in practice. Caroline Gipps (1988, p. 71) lists several 'generalizable characteristics which seem to be common to Primary schools today' on which 'regular and significant examining . . . will . . ., on the basis of what we know already about the effects of testing, have an impact'. What we are saying here is that that impact extends beyond certain aspects of primary practice to the very way in which the curriculum is conceived and, further, that this is a result not merely of testing *per se*, but of the form of testing adopted.

For it is important to remember that testing and assessment are not one and the same thing, and that testing is only one form of assessment. It is possible, therefore, to frame a programme of assessment and to devise instruments of assessment which will interlock with and provide support for a procedural or developmental approach to curriculum. It is even possible to frame attainment targets which are procedural and do not necessarily reflect an objectives model of curriculum. The attainment targets set by the Design and Technology Working Group are procedural in this way, listing aspects of capability rather than stages in a linear process of knowledge acquisition (reflecting perhaps the influence of the APU team) – identifying needs and opportunities, generating a design proposal, planning and making, evaluating, information technology capability. In this area at least, then, there is no mismatch with a process-based curriculum. In English too an attempt has been made to frame the attainment targets in terms of procedural capabilities and to employ profiling forms of assessment along the lines of the Inner London Education Authority's Primary Language Record to which reference was made earlier. In some other subject areas, however, as we have seen, the attainment targets are framed very much in terms of the 'knowledge, skills and understanding' which we are constantly hearing pupils need to acquire, so that attainment targets of this kind reflect a very different approach to assessment and thus 'lead' us to a very different concept of the curriculum itself – and, indeed, of education.

It is perhaps worth noting here that the professionals who are currently working to develop SATs at all levels are attempting to focus the assessment procedures on processes, especially by concentrating on those ATs which are expressed in process terms, even though they recognize the difficulties this creates in relation to the testing of knowledge-content. In particular, the team developing non-statutory SATs for design and technology at key stage 1 is following the example of the APU Design and Technology team and seeking to generate content-free SATs. Such a form of assessment, however, does not lend itself to short, sharp, pencil-and-paper tests nor to simplistic modes of interpretation and expression. Such tests, then, are not likely to prove acceptable to the politicians and the administrators, the new educrats. And there are already signs that these SATs will not be accepted and that some much more simplistic forms of testing will be required, found and implemented.

In exploring assessment in the early years, then, we need to look beyond statements of what it is intended to do, to the realities of the impact it is actually having or is likely to have. We must acknowledge the complex nature of the interrelationship of assessment and curriculum. We must accept the wisdom of the assertion that assessment must be 'the servant, not the master, of the curriculum'; and we must recognize the full import of that assertion, which is not only that we should plan our curriculum first and then devise forms of assessment to match it, but that those forms of assessment must match it in every respect, not merely in respect of its content but also, and more importantly, in respect of the fundamental way in which it is conceived. We must finally appreciate fully the effects of mismatch in this aspect of educational provision, and the results of attempting what is an impossible task, at both the practical and the conceptual levels, of matching a form of assessment based on one set of principles, on one concept of education, to a curriculum which is founded on something completely different. Again this is a problem which may have particular implications for, and create specially significant problems for, those concerned with the education of the under-fives, for whom a curriculum planned in terms of its subject content would seem not only inappropriate but even quite ridiculous, but who may well be subjected to this form of assessment, if only, as we are now told, to provide a yardstick for subsequent testing at 7+.

The attempt to impose this kind of assessment on children in the early years of their education must be attributable either to ignorance and an associated lack of conceptual clarity or to a deliberate intention to change the way in which the early years curriculum is conceived and planned. Again, if the latter is the case, it represents an emphasis on the use of assessment for summative and administrative purposes rather than for purposes which might be described as formative or educational. It can further be seen as an attempt to use assessment as a form of control; and this aspect of assessment deserves a brief examination before we bring this chapter to a close.

ASSESSMENT AS CONTROL

The briefest survey of the history of the development of public forms of assessment in the United Kingdom quickly reveals that their prime role has been administrative, and that it is not difficult to find the evidence which will take one beyond that and offer support to the claim that it has also been political, that assessment has been used as a device for social control.

It is not the intention here to offer a potted history of the development of examinations systems. It is worth reminding ourselves, however, that, until very recently, history reveals that the concern for, and the justification of, examination systems have derived entirely from the need for the selection and certification of pupils – for secondary education, for further/higher education and for employment. First introduced by Oxford and Cambridge Universities for the award of degrees, then used by professional bodies for acceptance into membership, then adopted for admission to military academies and the Civil Service, examinations slowly became a device for the issuing of certificates of all kinds – hence the School Certificate and Higher School Certificate, the General Certificate of Education at O- and A-level, the Certificate of Secondary Education and, since 1988, the common 16+ examination, the General Certificate of Secondary Education – not to mention the system of scholarships for admission to grammar schools which later became the 11+.

Throughout this time, however, equal concern has been expressed about the potentially anti-educational effects of examinations. The Taunton Report (1868), for example, suggested that it may be an inevitable effect of any examination system to be directive of the curriculum. This concern was reiterated more recently in the Beloe Report (SSEC, 1960). We might also note the claim of Matthew Arnold, in commenting on the Revised Code of 1862 and the system of 'payment by results' which it introduced, that 'examinations and payment by results deprived children of liberal education, and teachers of their rightful freedom' (Curtis and Boultwood, 1960, p. 142) and that what he observed in schools and attributed to that legislation was 'a deadness, a slackness, and a discouragement which are not the signs and accomplishments of progress' and 'a lack of intelligent life much more striking now than it was when I returned from the Continent in 1859' (Curtis, 1948, p. 263).

In spite of this, little attempt has been made until recently to suggest that examinations have, or might have, positive educational advantages, or that systems of assessment might be devised to contribute more positively to the quality of educational provision, by means other than checking on a limited range of 'standards'. They have thus traditionally been regarded as instruments of administration, necessary perhaps, even a necessary evil, but offering little, if anything, in the way of educational advantage. Thus their proven *raison d'être* has been their summative rather than their formative function, intentions and effects, and their role has been administrative, even political.

The introduction of formal, external assessment into early childhood education, and especially its introduction as a deliberately summative form of assessment, must represent an attempt to introduce administrative controls rather than to improve educational 'standards'. If the latter were the intention, then the process should have been accompanied by a deep exploration of the potential of other forms of assessment, those geared more positively to a diagnostic or formative function.

The last decade or so has seen much progress made towards the creation of forms of assessment which might be educationally supportive. We have already noted the progress made in this direction through the development of schemes of profiling and records of achievement. We may also note in this connection the major changes which have been associated with the introduction of the GCSE, changes which the statistics would seem to indicate have led already to improved standards. Those changes, however, require greater involvement of teachers and other associated professionals, and indeed of pupils themselves, in the assessment process; they involve greater freedom of interpretation at local level; they suggest a conceptualization of assessment as a matter of professional judgement rather than of measurement; they thus imply less centralized control.

We must, therefore, recognize the significance, as well as the impact, of the choice of a 'graded test' system of assessment for the National Curriculum rather than the kind of profiling or records of achievement which have been developing so rapidly, and indeed successfully, in recent years. It reflects a move back to a form of assessment whose focus, whatever its rhetoric, is on summative forms of assessment for increased administrative, and perhaps social, control. Its introduction in the early years of schooling considerably extends its influence and its sphere of control. It thus has many implications for those who are concerned with education in the early years, including those whose concern is with the under-fives. These will be explored more fully in subsequent chapters.

SUMMARY AND CONCLUSIONS

This chapter began by claiming that educational assessment is an imprecise activity, that it must depend to a great extent on judgement and that any use of the term 'measurement' in relation to educational assessment is metaphorical and probably misleading. It then went on to offer a brief overview of the several purposes of, dimensions of, approaches to, and indeed effects of assessment in education. It suggested that no scheme has been, nor perhaps could be, devised which will embrace or achieve all of these purposes, so that choices need to be made and priorities stated in relation to what we intend to achieve through our testing techniques, and thus, by inference, what we regard as of less importance. It indicated that in essence this choice lies between emphasizing the summative aspects of assessment, and thus its administrative and political purposes, and those educational purposes which are to be achieved by approaches which emphasize the formative dimensions. It also indicated that there are important and subtle relationships between assessment and curriculum and between forms of assessment and concepts of curriculum, and that the choice of the former has several implications for the nature of the latter, that the programme of assessment selected must either match or lead, and perhaps distort, the kind of curriculum we can offer.

The chapter finally noted that the history of the development of assessment systems in the United Kingdom reveals an emphasis on their summative functions, since they have all been devised and developed to achieve administrative, and sometimes political, ends. Only in recent years, through schemes for profiling and records of achievement, can one see serious and successful attempts being made to develop systems which emphasize the formative, the ipsative, the judgemental, the educational purposes that assessment might fulfil.

Attention was then drawn to the significance of the choice of the former approach in the planning of the National Curriculum testing programme, the adoption of a 'graded test' rather than a profiling scheme. For this, it was suggested, implies that the central purpose of this programme is administrative and political rather than educational.

This scheme, as we know only too well, has been extended also into the first school. Subsequent chapters will explore the particular implications of that.

2
PROGRESSION, OBSERVATION AND ASSESSMENT IN EARLY EDUCATION: THE CONTEXT

Geva Blenkin

Examinations are formidable even to the best prepared; for the greatest fool may ask more than the wisest man can answer.

(Charles Colton, 1780–1832)

It would have been unthinkable a decade ago for teachers of young children to consider that this quip had any serious significance for their professional work. They may have agreed with its basic premise and been amused by it. They may have recognized that assessment procedures can be unreliable and unfair. They may even have sympathized with colleagues who worked with older pupils and they may have agreed with them that the public examination system can be a major constraint on education in the later stages of schooling. They would almost certainly have been thankful, however, that such problems and preoccupations were outside their remit as early years educators, at least in any formal or public sense.

For children in Britain begin their compulsory schooling at a very young age compared to children elsewhere in the world, and this was seen as a good reason why early childhood education should be exempt from public examinations. During the period when the 11+ examination dominated the work of the primary sector of schooling, for example, the preparation of the children for the tests was contained within junior departments and even confined to the last year of the junior school. The effects of 11+ testing, therefore, had little impact on infant and nursery schools in the United Kingdom. Indeed, even during the short-lived Victorian system of 'payment-by-results' in the public sector of schooling, the youngest children – the babies and infants as they were then called – were not expected to demonstrate through their achievements the effectiveness of their teachers, although the top-down pressure to begin teaching the three Rs as early as possible was certainly present at the time (Whitbread, 1972).

As we saw in Chapter 1, however, all of this has changed with the arrival of the Education Reform Act of 1988. Assessment of the performance of all the six- and seven-year-olds who are at the end of their infant school education in England and Wales has been one of the main innovations, and one of the most controversial aspects, of this legislation (Pollard, 1990). For it has meant that early years teachers, or at least those who are working in infant schools, are now required to act formally as examiners of the educational performance of their pupils.

This requirement has forced assessment to the forefront of the debate about how young children can learn most effectively in school. To parents and politicians it is a simple matter. Tests will inform them of the progress made by children. Tests may also tell them about the effectiveness of teachers. History has shown, however, that such a simplistic view of assessment is likely to undermine the achievements of both the children and their teachers. The responsibility has fallen on professional teachers, therefore, to convince parents of this, while satisfying the reasonable wish of those parents to know how their children are progressing. To do this, however, teachers must understand the role of assessment in learning in some depth and they must also be able to explain assessment procedures and their effects to parents in a straightforward manner. The acquisition of this professional expertise and advocacy is one of the greatest challenges for educationists in the present day.

An essential first step towards such a professional understanding is to clarify the different concepts of assessment. In Chapter 1, for example, the dangers of an overemphasis on summative forms of assessment, especially in the early years of schooling, were outlined. It was argued there that teachers must be aware of the purposes and impact of assessment if young children's development is to be advanced and not constrained.

Theoretical understanding is of little professional use, however, if the practical implications of theories are not clarified. The next step towards a thorough understanding of assessment, therefore, is to identify and evaluate the different approaches that are currently adopted in early education in order to demonstrate, in the practical context, which approaches are most effective and defensible. It is the intention of this chapter, therefore, to complement the conceptual clarification that was undertaken in Chapter 1 by providing an overview and an evaluation of assessment practices in the early years.

The discussion will show that many approaches to assessment have been tried in schools and nursery centres, and it will be argued that often these have been adopted in an eclectic manner and with insufficient attention to the assumptions about teaching and learning that lie behind each procedure. They have been drawn, therefore, from a range of traditions, some of which run counter to the developmental view of education which is widely supported by early years teachers. The discussion will then turn to a consideration of the impact of these different procedures on the children themselves. Assessment of human learning is not merely a technical matter, for the system adopted will influence the relationship between the assessor and the one who is being assessed. And this will affect the results. It is important that teachers, parents and other concerned adults fully understand this effect and appreciate its significance, particularly when very young children are being assessed. Finally, the chapter will review developmental procedures for assessment in early education and emphasize the inter-personal nature of these assessments.

A main theme of the chapter is that effective assessment depends upon effective assessors. We must begin, therefore, by evaluating briefly the effectiveness of early years practitioners through a discussion of their responses to external demands for assessment.

ASSESSMENT IN THE NATIONAL CURRICULUM: TESTING TIMES

The Secretary of State may, by orders, specify in relation to each of the foundation subjects such attainment targets, such programmes of study and such assessment arrangements as he considers appropriate for that subject.
(The Education Reform Act 1988, Section 4)

The new Education Act was, at first, greeted with disbelief by early childhood educators both in Britain and abroad. Although the practical arrangements for assessment were not detailed in the Act, the centralized power that was evident and the subject-led curriculum that was implied both ran counter to the early years traditions.

This shift in emphasis was not totally unexpected. There had been a trend, for example, during the 1980s in many areas of the world, as well as in Britain, towards what has been described by two observers as 'the increased scrutiny of escalating educational expenditure, which is usually accompanied by calls for greater "accountability" and "measurability" ' (Carr and Claxton, 1989, p. 129). This trend was in turn accompanied by the worry, recognizable internationally, especially among early childhood educationists, that the consequent testing of pupil performance in school might run counter to what was most appropriate educationally for young children. What was unique in Britain, however, was that the testing was to be linked to a prescribed curriculum which was to be followed by all children in England and Wales at a younger age than children in schools elsewhere.

As the implications of both the National Curriculum, with its single subject approach, and the new assessment requirements became clearer, many teachers were plunged into gloom. Among the many difficulties that they faced was the fact that 'there was no piloting of the curriculum and teacher assessment procedures before making them legally binding' (Association for Science Education, 1990, p. 8). Concern was expressed, of course, about the dangers of involving very young children in inappropriate activities for the purposes of assessment. Perhaps the greatest irony of all, however, was that the teachers working at key stage 1 – that is, the teachers who had no tradition or experience in public examination procedures and who were also working with the youngest, most vulnerable pupils – were to be the pioneers of the new system.

There was one further aspect of the 1988 Education Reform Act that caused serious concern and was seen by many as likely to have more far-reaching effects on state education in the early years than even the curriculum and assessment requirements themselves. For the National Curriculum legislation applied only to the education of children of compulsory school age.

The immediate impact of this was twofold. First, it placed nursery education low on the political agenda, leaving nursery teachers in an even more marginal position within the teaching profession and increasing their feelings of isolation and of being undervalued. Second, it widened the gap between the practice of teachers in the nursery and the infant schools, and, in doing so, fractured what is acknowledged internationally as the distinctive phase of early childhood education.

In such uncertain and bewildering times, it was perhaps understandable that the first response of practitioners was, in Drummond's words, 'to close ranks, stick together and deny all knowledge of the profession's imperfections' (ibid., 1989, p. 8). The prospect of examinations in early childhood seemed to be particularly formidable, however well prepared the children were, and the future, therefore, seemed fraught with problems.

Such defensiveness on the part of practitioners may have been an inevitable response to the political context of these policies. It also revealed, however, a widespread insecurity amongst early years practitioners. For, although advances in professional theory and practice had been made prior to the Act, including advances in the understanding of assessment in education, these had not been implemented, or even understood, by many teachers.

An important reason for this was that a majority of teachers in training had not been encouraged to adopt a critical stance to their practice. Their training had been dominated, according to one historian, by a Froebelian tradition for much of the century, and the advocates of this tradition had reacted, too often, 'with closed minds' to other views (Whitbread, 1972, p. 59). This situation worsened as the government-controlled, subject-led teacher training was introduced and imposed during the 1980s. For this meant that many teachers were not helped to translate their own theory of teaching and learning into clear curricular terms, let alone recognize the conflicting features of competing theories (Blenkin, 1988). The style of these new courses of teacher training also meant that the study of child development was largely excluded from the initial training of early years teachers and was replaced by subject study.

As a result, teaching strategies were adopted uncritically and, in many schools, a range of theories of early education permeated practices, causing confusion and distortion. Nowhere was this more evident than in relation to assessment, for assessment procedures have a powerful influence on practice, on the curriculum and on the children themselves (Broadfoot, 1979). And, when they are adopted uncritically, they can become the most potent source of the distortion of practice (Tizard *et al.*, 1988).

The classroom studies of the 1970s and 1980s had revealed many such distortions and many instances where teachers' practices were in conflict with their ideas about educating young children (King, 1978; Tizard and Hughes, 1984; Wells, 1986). It became clear that a large number of early years teachers, like their colleagues in other sectors of the schooling system, had great difficulty in relating theory to practice. This in turn meant that they had difficulty in explaining and justifying early education practices to parents and to others. Their professional language rarely went beyond the pedagogic romanticism of the Plowden Report (CACE, 1967), and they were vulnerable, as a result, to the retrogressive policies which were being introduced into schools (Alexander, 1984; Simon, 1985).

It was unfortunate that, at a time when radical legislation was being introduced to change the education system in England and Wales, professional confidence was being undermined even further by the findings of these studies. The studies also revealed, however, that some teachers in early education had made progress in developing both an appropriate curriculum for the young child and assessment procedures that would be compatible with this curriculum. The reasons for this progress became a major focus of professional interest.

Progression, observation and assessment of both children's development and of teachers' effectiveness in promoting that development had been recurring themes in early childhood education during most of the twentieth century. Professional studies of these themes had been informed, throughout this long period, by widespread research into early human learning which had been conducted in related disciplines – notably in developmental or cognitive psychology. The insights gained from these sources into the assessment of children's development had not, until recently, been constrained by externally imposed structures. As a result, a strong tradition of ensuring progression in young children's learning by using assessment procedures based on observational strategies had been established. This meant that the evaluation and the assessment procedures practised in some nursery and infant schools were developing hand-in-hand, and had advanced, as was noted in Chapter 1, to a more sophisticated and sensitive level than had happened elsewhere in the schooling system.

At first, this advanced professional practice was labelled as 'good' practice which was attainable only by 'gifted' practitioners. A closer analysis of such practice was under way, however, both in Britain and abroad, and, as we will see in later chapters, it was already being translated into defensible professional terms and into a language which was understandable to teachers and parents alike. These practices were being disseminated, therefore, to a wider range of schools and nursery centres.

This brief appraisal of the effectiveness of practitioners at this testing time certainly reveals many anomalies. On the one hand, it shows many instances of professional imperfections, especially in the area of assessment. These are evident in the studies of teachers at work, for example, and in the apparent inability of the profession to convince parents that simple tests at 7+ will be of little educational use and might even be bad for children. On the other hand, however, there is clear evidence of significant advances made by many ordinary teachers in the implementation of the best assessment practices.

Apart from creating an awareness of these anomalies, however, the legislation has produced one further important response from the profession. For it has pressed most early years practitioners into the view that professionals, as well as politicians and parents, need to be clearer about the ways in which children's development can be assessed. If simplistic modes of assessment are to be rejected, then more appropriate procedures must be found to replace them. These procedures may well be part of current practices but, if parents and others are to be convinced of their value, they will need to be made more apparent in that practice. This will require some clear thinking about the weaknesses as well as the strengths of these current practices. One way of embarking upon such reflection and clarification is to consider how current practices came about.

THE EVOLUTION OF ASSESSMENT IN EARLY CHILDHOOD EDUCATION

Monday, 28 February . . .

Jack, meanwhile, had been filling page after page with his 'writing' . . . He numbered the pages, following a list I wrote out for him. Inevitably, he made a mistake. He called for my liquid Tipp-Ex . . . and though he applied it very liberally he could not completely eradicate a badly deformed '5'. He became upset and nothing I could say dissuaded him from ripping out all the pages he had written and crumpling them up.

It was a common complaint among the kids at the school where I worked last year that writing was difficult because you could not help making mistakes which spoilt the look of what you had done; they were quite unconcerned about the meaning of what they had put down. They too were lavish users of Tipp-Ex.

Sadly, Jack is far less able than Tilly to get pleasure from his writing and drawing; more often than not he ends up destroying his work. I hope for his sake this is only a phase.

(Harrison, 1985, p. 251)

A Father's Diary, from which the above extract is taken, never fails to delight both parents and teachers of young children. The diary preserves details and incidents during one year in the life of Tilly, aged four, and her three-year-old brother, Jack; and this, in itself, is fascinating. Its real strength, however, lies in the honesty of the father's account and the way in which his recording of everyday incidents offers an insight into the workings of the young children's minds. For example, the entries about their early attempts to read and write highlight graphically the real interests and anxieties that these activities provoke in children. Those passages also reveal the distinctly different styles and responses of the two children to the challenges of becoming literate.

This record was not written for the purposes of assessing the children, of course, although Fraser Harrison admits in his introduction that one reason for keeping the diary was to enable him to reflect on his own effectiveness as a father. The intimate account of this family's life in the Suffolk countryside tells us much, however, about Tilly's and Jack's development during the year. It also offers general insights into the many ways in which young children learn as they cope with the normal routines and happenings of daily life. It is this narrative approach to record-keeping which emerged nearly a century ago in early childhood education, and has had a profound and persistent influence on assessment ever since.

Early traditions

It is not surprising that the tradition of studying children through naturalistic accounts has such a long history in early education and is still so appealing to teachers and other professionals who are concerned with the very young. At such an early stage in their lives, children are not readily able to oblige those who are interested in assessing their progress by engaging in paper and pen or pencil exercises or by producing the other artefacts that are used to assess the progress of older children. Early years practitioners had to find alternative ways of understanding and charting development.

It was at the turn of the century that teachers in the United States recognized that they shared this problem with members of the new disciplines of psychology, and they were particularly interested in the work of developmental and cognitive psychologists. It was through this mutual interest in child watching that the Child Study movement was born and the connection between developmental psychology and early education was made (Johnson, 1988).

It was a powerful and persistent connection as far as assessment was concerned, for it placed the issues of both curriculum provision and assessment in the context of the children's own development. This meant that, to use the terms explored in Chapter 1, it was ipsative assessment, rather than either norm-referenced or criterion-referenced assessments, that came to be dominant in early childhood education. These assessments were concerned as much with deducing how young children learn and how learning could be advanced more effectively, as they were with how the young child being assessed was progressing.

The move in this direction was further encouraged in Britain by the work of Susan Isaacs at her Malting House School during the 1920s. Her analysis of the detailed observations that had been collected there led her to the view that individual differences in development were of great significance. She also argued strongly for the value of qualitative and holistic records, and cautioned against observations which are too reliant on a predetermined plan or system. In her view, qualitative records were 'not only . . . an essential preliminary to fruitful experiment in genetic psychology, but . . .

may well remain an indispensable background and corrective, even when experimental technique is perfected' (Isaacs, 1933, p. 4). Her contribution was to introduce a more structured and scientific approach to holistic and qualitative observations, and to encourage early years practitioners to appreciate the value of individual records which were personal and not systematized.

By the middle of the century, the Child Study movement, with its developmental approach, had established its dominance among early years practitioners. Approaches to assessment from other traditions, however, were also emerging and establishing themselves.

Susan Isaacs' argument in favour of qualitative observations, for example, was mounted largely to challenge a second tradition, that of behaviourism, which was becoming fashionable at the time (Whitbread, 1972). An approach similar to that of the behaviourists had been adopted by Maria Montessori. For, although she had pioneered the introduction of informal activities in early education, these were structured in a graded sequence and were always guided by adults.

Maria Montessori was suspicious of fantasy and socio-dramatic play, seeing them as 'an undesirable escape from reality' (Smith, 1988, p. 211). She preferred instead real-life activities such as cooking and gardening to be encouraged, and limited the children's play to using structured materials. Her 'didactic material', as she called her play objects, was designed to train the mind and the senses in a predetermined manner, and she explains her method in the following passage:

> Our didactic material renders auto-education possible, permits a methodological education of the senses. Not upon the ability of the teacher does education rest, but upon the didactic system. This presents objects which, first, attract the spontaneous attention of the child, and, second, contain a rational gradation of stimuli.
>
> (Montessori, 1912, p. 175)

She too encouraged teachers to keep detailed, individual records of the children. These observations, however, were not holistic but were structured with reference to the 'rational gradation' of her system. They were, in other words, criterion-referenced, and the criteria used were behavioural.

The systematic planning of learning programmes which had built-in assessment criteria was mainly developed, however, in the United States by behavioural psychologists. There was the same resistance, at first, to this approach in the mainstream of early education in Britain as there had been to the Montessori method. Behavioural techniques were adopted and popularized, however, by those working with handicapped children, and especially by educational psychologists, whose training tended to be in child psychology rather than in child development, and who were working in the health sector rather than the education sector of public service, and were not influenced, therefore, by mainstream thinking about early education.

The behavioural approach was well established in the United States by the time that Ralph Tyler's seminal text, 'Basic Principles of Curriculum and Instruction', was published in 1949. The Tylerian influence became most apparent in Britain with the publication of the Warnock Report (DES, 1978), which commended the objectives approach to planning and assessment for children with learning difficulties and argued that 'it is now recognized that the tasks and skills to be learned by these children have to be analysed precisely and that the setting of small, clearly defined, incremental objectives for individual children is a necessary part of programme planning (op. cit., p. 221).

The behavioural approach had also been influential in a less overt way, however, during the period when large-scale curriculum projects were sponsored in the United Kingdom during the 1960s and 1970s. In the early stages of what has come to be known as 'the curriculum development movement', project directors adopted an American approach to the planning and evaluation of their projects. Most soon rejected this approach, however, on the grounds that it was either unworkable or undesirable for the development of education projects (Stenhouse, 1980).

The legacy nevertheless persisted in early childhood education, and was particularly influential in projects which addressed the issue of the assessment of children. In the three projects in this field – Assessment in Nursery Education (Bate and Smith, 1978), Keele Pre-School Assessment (Tyler, 1980) and Record-Keeping in Primary Schools (Clift, Weiner and Wilson, 1981) – for example, behavioural techniques are evident in the taxonomies that were devised, the objectives which were set and the performance tasks that were advocated. The guides from these projects were used widely, especially in nurseries, by teachers and nursery officers who were still claiming to support a child-led curriculum. The use of criterion-referenced and graded tests at key stage 1 of the National Curriculum is further evidence of the influence of behaviourism.

Practitioners in the early years, however, showed an awareness of and, often, a dislike of the third tradition that emerged in the early part of the century. The psychometric tradition had gained popularity in other sectors of schooling, especially after the creation of a separate system of secondary education, when standardized tests were used at 11+ to sort and select children for allocation to 'appropriate' secondary schools. These tests were welcomed, as they seemed to give an air of fairness to these selection procedures.

Intelligence tests, of the kind employed in the selection procedures at 11+, were never used widely by teachers in nursery and infant schools, however, as the need for selection according to ability was not institutionalized in the early years. This does not mean, however, that such selection did not occur. Many preparatory schools in the private sector, for example, conducted tests before children were accepted. It was also clear, from a survey conducted in the late 1970s, that standardized tests, especially of reading ability, were most frequently in use in maintained schools at the beginning as well as at the end of the junior school (Gipps *et al.*, 1983). When the Schonell Graded Word Reading Test was published in 1955, reading became the skill that was most widely tested by the use of norm-referenced procedures.

Screening techniques, conducted mainly by educational psychologists, relied heavily on standardized tests to identify children's particular difficulties in the early years, but these were restricted to children whose development was clearly delayed. In 1975, however, the Bullock Report (DES, 1975) recommended that nursery and infant teachers should be fully involved in screening, to identify all children 'at risk' as early as possible in their schooling. While expressing doubts about the setting of standardized tests for all children at seven, the committee came out in favour of screening tests that 'combine simplicity of operation with a recognition of the holistic nature of language learning' and 'have been developed and evaluated within the last ten years' (op. cit., p. 249). The Cockcroft enquiry into mathematics similarly supported early screening of pupils to identify difficulties, but the committee cautioned that 'standardized tests measure only some aspects of mathematical attainment', and recommended that 'when the results of standardized tests are used . . . these results should not be used by themselves' (DES, 1982, p. 123).

During the 1970s, practitioners were being involved more and more in the screening of children to identify those with 'special needs', and assessment was focusing increasingly on management issues rather than on issues that related to individual development. Norm-referenced, standardized tests seemed to be more acceptable to practitioners if used in these circumstances. As one observer argues, 'the efficacy of screening techniques lies less in their ability in a fine-grained way to assess individual functioning than in being a local survey tool for planning purposes' (Wolfendale, 1989, p. 113). Indeed, the recent interest in 'baseline' assessment on the part of early years teachers has signalled a change in attitude to the psychometric tradition. It also relates more to teacher protection than to child development.

The three traditions that have been considered so far all evolved slowly throughout the century. The Child Study movement remained dominant for most of this period. Early years practitioners adopted behavioural and psychometric techniques, however, as more precision in assessment was demanded, especially from those outside the profession, even though, as we saw in Chapter 1, such precision is a chimera. And as the calls for 'structure' and 'screening' came to the fore, it was claimed that the Child Study approach was structureless and consequently unable to meet external demands. Other traditions seemed to offer the required structure and precision, and many practitioners turned to these as a result, without considering the effects that this might have on their practice.

It was the issue of structure, however, that also introduced the fourth tradition of assessment into early education. The developmental or constructivist tradition grew out of the Child Study movement. It began to promote a more structured approach to child watching, however, especially when the research studies of Jean Piaget were translated into English and began to influence teacher-training institutions in both Britain and the United States during the 1960s. Constructivist research methods, such as those of Piaget, were designed to investigate the 'match' or 'mismatch' between, on the one hand, children's levels of understanding and, on the other, the concepts from different areas of human understanding (Athey, 1990). There was, therefore, an obvious link between the techniques that were developed for psychological investigations and those that were required by teachers for assessment purposes.

As I have argued elsewhere (Blenkin, 1988), these links were made in a direct and naive way at first. It became common practice, for example, to 'test' young children's thinking by re-running the classic Piagetian experiments in early years classrooms. This led, at first, to undesirable results which seemed to lead researchers and teachers to a deterministic view of development and a deficit view of young children's abilities (Donaldson, 1978).

As techniques were perfected, however, they were translated into clearer professional terms, especially in certain areas of human development and understanding. Chris Athey argues, for example, that 'greatest progress has been made in "matching" curriculum content with cognitive form in mathematics and science. Constructivist research into early literacy has also produced new information on young children's understanding of language' (Athey, 1990, p. 16).

An important issue that was addressed by the adherents of this tradition was the kinds of structure that should be adopted in observation and assessment. In this work they were influenced by Vygotsky's ideas, and in particular by his notion of 'the zone of proximal development' (Vygotsky, 1978). Criteria for assessment were needed but, if these were linked too closely to content or performance, they would become too deterministic and closed, and the social interactions and other contextual features of the learning situation would be ignored or discounted. This would make the results of the assessments inaccurate and misleading.

For these reasons, it was argued that assessment criteria should be developmental and not behavioural or identified too closely with the mastery of content. Developmental criteria were structured by reference to 'forms of representation' of experience rather than to subjects or skills (Eisner, 1982). This made them more open and made it more possible to appreciate the personal responses of the children to the activities that were to be assessed. It was also recommended that assessments of a more structured kind should always be backed by more long-term, holistic records of development and achievement which would act as a further corrective (Wolf, 1988).

This brief reflection on the emergence of these different traditions of assessment in early education shows that, like other aspects of educational provision and curriculum planning, the early years approach is related to, but distinct from, the style adopted in other sectors of the schooling system. Assessment techniques were introduced in the early years with less deliberation, for example. They evolved slowly, therefore, and influenced practices in a range of ways. There were positive influences, which produced highly advanced professional practice. There were also, however, negative influences, which often produced confusion in practice. Finally, the discussion has revealed that, despite claims to the contrary from politicians and others, all concepts of assessment are present, to some degree, in the practices of early education. We must end this section by summarizing the ways in which emerging influences and approaches have been formalized and have produced the recognizable professional procedures of the present day.

Formalized approaches

(a) Norm-referenced assessment

It was suggested above that early years practitioners have tended to resist norm-referenced approaches to assessment. Standardized tests, including

IQ tests, have been, and are still being, used in the assessment of young children whose development is severely delayed, but it was not until the period when the screening of reading performance was advocated that norm-referenced tests began to be adopted widely by teachers, especially at the end of the infant school. Children's reading ages are now commonly tested at seven, as part of the preparation for transfer to the junior school.

Indeed, standardized tests at seven have been popularized by a majority of local education authorities and have been extended to include mathematics and verbal reasoning as well as reading. In a recent research study (Gipps *et al.*, 1983), for example, it was shown that testing programmes had been introduced by many local education authorities for three main reasons. There were political reasons – to ensure that the authorities were forearmed in the event of questions about standards. There were organizational reasons – to enable issues of provision and transfer to be resolved. And there were professional reasons – to facilitate the early identification of weaknesses in the performance of individuals and groups of children. The research team argued, therefore, that 'these categories result in testing programmes of three major types: monitoring programmes for accountability purposes, testing for transfer and screening programmes' (op. cit., p. 32). Standardized tests were important in each of these three categories of programme.

This well-established pattern in many local education authorities is now being formalized nationally through the SATs at key stage 1. It is not insignificant that many parents and politicians, as well as teachers, are calling for simpler standardized tests in reading and number to replace the rather cumbersome SATs that have been developed so far. Standardized tests are also recommended by some teachers at the 'baseline' age of five years, as we saw in Chapter 1, so that progress made by children during the time when teachers can influence that progress may be measured.

As we will see later in this chapter, however, a majority of early years teachers are still at the forefront in arguing that standardized tests that are administered at such a young age are undesirable. Although tests might be objected to, the use of reading schemes as a means of deducing standardization of performance has been accepted by many infant teachers during most of this century, and many are now using mathematics schemes in a similar manner.

(b) Criterion-referenced assessment

Schemes and programmes have also been influential in promoting criterion-referenced tests and assessment in early education. For criterion-referenced assessments have tended, so far, to use either behavioural or subject-centred approaches or both. This means that they have depended on material that will encourage children to demonstrate both their level of performance and their mastery of content. Criterion-referencing has also come to the fore with the introduction of the objectives-based and subject-based National Curriculum.

This approach to assessment has been a long-established tradition in the early years, however, as was noted earlier. The three projects on assessment that were cited above adopted criterion-referenced techniques and demonstrate the two main difficulties with this approach. First, the record-schedules are unwieldy because of the level of detail at which criteria need to be specified in order to describe and do justice to a child's performance. And, second, the profiles seem to be trivial and to leave out the most important aspects of the child's achievements, as these are difficult to specify, especially in terms of subject mastery.

The following extract illustrates these two points. It is taken from the Keele Pre-School Assessment Guide (Tyler, 1980, p. 30).

SECTION II

Read the items listed below and tick those which the child performs easily or frequently according to the criteria given in the manual. In the section on play patterns (S2) the child's ability rather than his usual performance should be recorded. Thereafter, shade in those sections on the chart corresponding to the items marked. The skills have been arranged in the approximate order of their normal development and mastery of the more advanced skills in the outer levels will usually succeed the acquisition of the skills occupying the inner rings. However, the assessor should not assume that this is always the case and care should be taken at all stages of the assessment.

(For definition of the items below refer to the accompanying manual)

COGNITION

C1.   Space and Time.

☐ 1. Differentiates night and day.
☐ 2. Matches patterned arrangements.
☐ 3. Knows some names of the days of the week.
☐ 4. Differentiates between left and right.
☐ 5. Knows today, tomorrow and yesterday.

C2.   Properties of Objects.

☐ 1. Can differentiate objects by size.
☐ 2. Can differentiate by weight.

☐ 3. Can distinguish elementary properties of materials (soft/hard, etc.).
☐ 4. Understands concepts of sinking and floating.
☐ 5. Conserves continuous quantity.

C3. Sorting and Classification Skills.

☐ 1. Can match by colour.
☐ 2. Can classify by colour.
☐ 3. Can perform 2-way classification.
☐ 4. Can arrange in order of size and insert in series.
☐ 5. Can perform simple set discrimination.

The experience of teachers who have used observation schedules and tick-lists such as these confirms that they are unsatisfactory. It often leads these teachers to report, for example, their concern that the most significant developments made by the children are not recorded, as these cannot be defined simplistically. In Desmond Nuttall's words (1990, p. 12), 'there is a great danger of fragmentation into discrete objectives, often low level because they are the easiest to specify, with the loss of high level and integrating objectives'.

As long as criterion-referencing remains inextricably linked to objectives approaches, to behaviourism and to subject-content this trivialization of educational assessments will be a persistent problem (Barrs, 1990). Criterion-referencing is an approach, however, that is gaining in popularity as modern computer technology aids the development and the perfection of 'item banks' of tests – standardized and inevitably criterion-referenced. Despite attempts to perfect techniques, however, infant teachers are already reporting, at the time of this writing, that the administration of SATs to seven-year-olds is a waste of teaching time, as they do not tell the teachers anything about the children that they did not already know and what they tell to those outside the school is barely worth knowing.

Even more worrying is the likelihood that the administration of these blanket tests to all children at key stage 1 will have the effect of depressing rather than raising standards of achievement. For, as two researchers have pointed out, 'much of the evidence from other countries suggests that attainment targets, when designed for a whole population of school pupils of a given age, are more likely to decrease expectations, have a harmful and restricting influence on teaching approaches, and generally lower educational standards rather than raising them' (Murphy and Torrance, 1988, p. 105).

There is one further significant area of early years work which is worth noting where criterion-referencing is being formalized, and this is in the validation of training courses. For criterion-referenced schedules, especially those that use performance indicators, are now being recommended for the assessment of early years practitioners as well as for the assessment of the children themselves.

(c) Ipsative assessment

It is clear from the summary above that criterion-referenced assessment is dominant, at present, in the formal procedures that are being introduced in Britain in conjunction with the National Curriculum. It is also interesting that, at exactly the same time, the case against such an approach to assessment is being argued elsewhere in the world.

In the United States, for example, where behavioural approaches have been most thoroughly tested, both in theory and in practice, the limitations and adverse effects of these have become very apparent, so that there other techniques are being sought. And it is qualitative approaches that are being explored and adopted in order to avoid the undesirable effects of the criterion- and norm-referenced tests that have been widely used in schools. As Dennie Palmer Wolf explains, 'the lack of powerful qualitative information about student learning, thoughtful ways of using that information, and training for educators in this kind of assessment is a major gap in the way American educators go about indexing and studying student learning' (Wolf, 1987, p. 26). She goes on to argue that the real understandings and genuine developments of students are not revealed by the assessments undertaken in schools because 'the grades, test scores, even samples of student work . . . are highly structured, product-oriented, and closed to students' (ibid.). In short, the structures that appear to be so appealing at present in Britain are being seen as ineffective, even undesirable, elsewhere.

Far from being structureless, the qualitative assessments that have been so influential in early education are now recognized as having their own structures. These are judgemental, however, rather than technical or even metric, as we saw in Chapter 1 all educational assessment must ultimately be. They are dependent, therefore, on informed assessors who are able to interpret observations and samples of children's work. The structures are also developmental rather than product-oriented. They focus on processes rather than on products or content. They are, therefore, more open and responsive to all the factors which might have relevance for the assessment.

Most progress in formalizing this kind of ipsative assessment has been made in relation to development in language and literacy. In building up a comprehensive and holistic picture of the child's progress in talking, reading and writing, several strategies have been adopted. Diaries that are shared between teacher and parent have provided detailed observations of the child's experiences as well as progress (Hannon *et al.*, 1985). Portfolios containing annotated examples of the child's early attempts at mark-making and writing have provided further longitudinal evidence. Modern technology, in particular tape and video-recorders, has extended this observational evidence to talking and learning. In addition, more structured approaches to observations of the child, such as miscue analysis in reading, have been introduced as more evidence from research becomes available.

All of these factors have helped to structure the records kept by teachers. These records, in turn, lend support to the merits of teacher assessment, for they deepen teachers' understanding of children and their development. They also inform the judgements that teachers make of the children's progress in learning.

In the Primary Language Record (CLPE, 1988), for example, which is the most advanced guide to the assessment of learning processes that is currently available, assessment strategies are, on occasions, focused and detailed, and yet they can be conducted on a day-to-day basis as part of normal classroom routines. The children's development in language and literacy is, therefore, charted in natural settings as part of the whole educational experience that is provided by teachers and parents. Perhaps most significant of all is that in developmental assessments, such as those advocated in the Primary Language Record, the child is an active participant in the assessment process.

This takes us, then, to a consideration of the most important aspect of the context of assessment in early education. For all assessments of children will have a significant impact on the children themselves. It is important, therefore, to clarify what is known about these effects as very young children are being exposed, increasingly, to forms of institutionalized assessment.

CHILDREN OR PUPILS? THE IMPACT OF ASSESSMENT

'Why do you keep asking the kids questions when you knows all the answers? Like . . . like . . . what colour is it then? You can see for yourself it's red . . . so why do you keep asking them?' Sonnyboy, aged five.

(Cousins, 1990, p. 30)

When children start school at three or five, their first major task is to learn to be a pupil. One of the most perplexing features of adopting this role is making sense of the behaviour of their teachers, especially as they attempt to assess their learning. Sonnyboy, speaking with great eloquence and the unflinching honesty of the young child, voices the dilemma faced by all children. As Cousins notes in her report of the Early Years Language Project, 'He wasn't being cheeky. He simply couldn't understand many of the rituals which either went on, or were talked about in the reception class' (op. cit., 1990, p. 30).

At this time, as the assessments at key stage 1 are being conducted, most adults who have close contact with young children are readily able to produce anecdotal evidence of this confusion or anxiety on the part of the children. There is Sarah, aged six, for example, who after school pursues her mother around the home as she does her chores, and insists, 'Mummy, we *must* do the National Curriclium tonight'. And Matilda who, at five, reported to her grandmother that the science project was boring and, when it was suggested to her that she should tell her teacher that she wasn't enjoying her task, responded 'Oh, no! Miss A has enough to worry about at the moment'. Unlike Sonnyboy, most children will remain silent about the confusing aspects of school, and this reticence, in turn, may lead teachers to underestimate their abilities as talkers and learners.

Cousins argues that this was a major problem in the reception classes that she studied. Confused children became silent or disruptive children, and their teachers 'dismissed the notion that there might have been transitional difficulties', and blamed, instead, 'the inadequacies of the children's working-class homes' (Cousins, 1990, p. 31).

There are at least four points of great significance to early learning in these anecdotes and in more formal studies of this kind.

First, there is the model of learning, and of schools, which is being offered to pupils at a time when they are learning to be pupils. That model is of learning as preparation for testing and of schools as places which seek to discover not only what you can do but also, and more threateningly, what you cannot.

Second, there is the reaction which this encourages in large numbers of children. For the question-and-answer mode of discourse in schools, which is prompted by this form of testing or assessment, has also been shown to create 'a context of disaffection' for many young children and to lead to 'the withdrawal of good will to engage in and learn from the adult world of compulsory schooling' (Barrett, 1989, p. xiv). Such studies of children's responses to school are particularly disturbing when set against the findings of more than 400 studies of the effects of teacher expectations on pupil progress. In reviewing these studies Rogers (1989) argues that inappropriate labelling of young children by teachers has a profound effect on success or failure which persists throughout their school career.

Third, we must note that this kind of reaction is much more likely to be found amongst pupils who come to school already lacking some of the advantages that make for smooth success in this kind of system – those from lower socio-economic backgrounds, for example, or from ethnic minority groups, for whom the ethos of schooling, its values and its practices may be somewhat at odds with the attitudes they bring with them, in short, those children for whom learning to be pupils is a major task. To reinforce this kind of conflict rather than seeking to alleviate it is to invite the kind of disaffection and 'switching-off' that studies have shown to occur. It is thus hardly conducive to raising standards in the case of these large cohorts of children.

Fourth, the adoption of this kind of approach to assessment in the early years invites teachers into different, and less helpful or supportive, attitudes towards their charges. For it encourages them to ask questions about children's work and progress of a kind rather more closely geared to making statements to the outside world, to responding to demands for teacher appraisal and accountability in relation to their own performance than to supporting pupils' progress in learning – questions with a summative rather than a formative emphasis. It thus leads them into taking the same limited view of learning and of education which is taken by those who press such assessment systems on them.

This kind of testing, then, can be seen to have adverse effects on pupils, on teachers and on the interaction between them, and to result in the creation of a context for learning which presents a less than helpful and supportive model of learning to both parties in the process. Conversely, we can learn from it more positive lessons about the kinds of assessment procedures which will genuinely support educational development, raise standards in the fullest sense of that term and help teachers to create a climate for learning which will offer encouragement to all pupils, whatever their background.

Finally, we must consider the adverse effects of this kind of testing which have just been outlined against the claim of its advocates that, nevertheless, it provides a fair and objective measurement of pupils' achievement. First, we must remember all that has been said, in the first two chapters of this book and in many other places, about the illusory nature of this presumed 'objectivity', the problematic aspects of the concept of 'educational measurement' and the manifest inaccuracies of all attempts to engage in it. Second, it is important to bear in mind that much of this inaccuracy is a result of the fact that all such tests are themselves clearly unfair, since they place at a disadvantage, as we have just seen, and as has been fully demonstrated by research studies (Gipps *et al.*, 1983), certain large categories of children. Third, even if they could provide such objective measurements, we would need to recognize that they did so at a cost – the cost of those distorting effects we have just noted – so that we would need to consider whether that is a price we are, or even should be, prepared to pay. And finally, we must return to the claim that the nearest we can get to fairness and objectivity in the assessment of children, especially in the early years, is to rely on the informed, professional judgements of those who know them, because they work closely with them, and who can thus take full account of the individuality, the idiosyncrasy and the subtlety of each child's development.

SUMMARY AND CONCLUSIONS

This chapter has sought to complement the conceptual review of assessment offered in Chapter 1 by exploring the context within which assessment in the early years has developed and the empirical evidence of the impact and effects of different forms of, and approaches to assessment.

It began by outlining the different theoretical stances which traditionally have influenced both approaches to the practice of education in the early years and to the assessment of pupils' development at this stage. It revealed that, just as teachers' practice and curriculum planning has often shown a confused response to conflicting and incompatible theoretical pressures and influences, so have the forms of assessment they have adopted. What also became clear, however, was that, as these theoretical positions have been progressively clarified in recent years, so have the techniques of assessment associated with them, and from this process a clearer view has emerged of the kinds of assessment which are necessary to support a genuinely developmental form of curricular provision.

The chapter then went on to consider some aspects of the impact of other, simpler forms of testing on pupils, teachers and schools. It revealed the limitations that such forms place on the way in which learning in the early years is conceived – by pupils as well as teachers – and highlighted the distorting effects such forms of testing can have on educational provision. In short, it showed some of what it means for the curriculum to be assessment-led, especially when the form of assessment which leads the curriculum is narrow and simplistic, so that the curriculum becomes effectively test-led.

Conversely, the chapter has also revealed some of the features of forms of assessment which can be extended and built upon to support a genuinely developmental approach to education in the early years. Subsequent chapters will elaborate on those features, while also offering further evidence of the inadequacies of the simple forms of testing currently being advocated.

3
ASSESSMENT AND THE NURSERY CURRICULUM

Victoria Hurst and Margaret Lally

Assessment is the most important professional area of a teacher's work. There is no other professional process in which the efficacy of the teacher and of the school can be so rigorously tested. Properly understood, assessment puts the achievement of the learner at the centre of the educational process, although not all approaches would have it this way. In fact, assessment is a highly controversial area, as may be seen from an examination of the educational areas to which it can be linked and for which it provides a reasoned critique.

Teachers have a responsibility for developing education (both in terms of provision and in terms of ideas about what constitutes educational quality) according to their understanding and experience. Assessment of children at any stage gives teachers information about the effectiveness of educational processes and procedures. This knowledge can then be applied to the working out of suitable provision for the future (the curriculum), and to the evaluation of educational ideas through critical analysis of their effects on learners.

Assessment is closely related, in these ways, to the evolution of ideas about educational quality as well as to the development of appropriate curricula. The progress of individual learners is vitally important to themselves and to their parents; it is important to teachers because it provides the surest footing for any self-evaluation and offers justification for their work when it is appraised; it is important to education because it offers ways in which to construct an educational critique of proposals or procedures.

THE ACTIVE ROLE OF THE TEACHER IN CURRICULUM DEVELOPMENT

Traditionally, teachers have been placed in a passive position in relation to research. They are frequently studied as objects rather than treated as active participants in research projects. They are also expected to apply in the classroom research solutions engendered elsewhere. This situation need not be accepted in that educational research problems are those encountered by teachers in classrooms inhabited by children, and there is no reason why teachers should not play a more active role in furthering professional knowledge.

(Athey, 1990, p. 19.)

The role that today's teachers can play in educational development is a leading one. In spite of hopeful pronouncements in connection with assessment for the National Curriculum, nobody knows how to monitor how children learn. Nobody knows what makes some children learn while others do not, or if they do they have not found how to incorporate this knowledge into curriculum development and from there into educational policy. We need to learn about children's learning and to learn how we can make better provision for teaching them.

Educational reasons are the only rational foundation for educational decisions. Our knowledge of the way that children learn should be the determining force in educational policy, and the fact that educational policy evolves while we are in a state of ignorance about learning weakens everything we do.

There is another dangerous area of ignorance in education. The problem of educational 'failure to thrive' has been a source of public concern for many years; it has been with us as an urgent issue since the Newsom Report drew public attention to it in the 1960s, and yet we are not much nearer to resolving it in spite of our efforts. Anxiety about the large numbers of pupils who leave school at the earliest opportunity is equalled by concern about the significant numbers who leave with inadequate educational achievements, and about those whose school careers seem characterized by alienation and failure (Hurst, 1991, ch. 6).

PERSONAL ASSESSMENT AND EQUAL OPPORTUNITIES

Lally (1991) explores how it is the task of the nursery teacher to be aware of children's personal experiences and needs as the pivotal point around which the curriculum must centre if each child is to have personal educational opportunities. It is our contention here that personal assessment is the way in which this responsibility can be carried out. It is the only way in which teachers can know the children they teach well enough to make provision for the needs of each. Without this knowledge, the provision may be well intentioned yet particular children may be disadvantaged by it.

Concern for equal opportunities has led to an examination of structures, institutions and attitudes (see, for instance, Browne and France, eds., 1986). Simultaneously, we can provide a critique of provision for actual children by investigating the match between their personal assessments and the curriculum provided. In order to do this, however, we need to know the children and their classrooms very well indeed.

TEACHERS AND RESEARCH

The teachers, who see children's learning in operation, are the people who are in the best position to spot effective pedagogic strategies and to evolve theories to explain their effectiveness. From the theories we can develop pedagogical foundations for ideas about what the curriculum should be. During the last decade, teachers have focused their attention on collaboration with parents, and the success of home-school reading schemes has been such that the strategy has been extended to mathematics as well (Merttens and Vass, 1990b). The primary curriculum has been influenced by these developments and there is now much more understanding of the need to work from children's experiences at home and in the community in order to facilitate children's acquisition of concepts. How this is to be done must depend on what we know about each child.

Learning about literacy from a child

For example, Kerry, aged three years two months, set off to 'go to the shops', pushing a friend in the pram. Part-way into the playground she stopped, and went to fetch paper and pencil 'to make a list'. The list that she made had zigzag lines, one under another, with a few capital Ks and Rs at the side. This observation enabled the teacher to assess Kerry's understanding of the place of literacy in daily life and to see how she could be helped to extend her understanding. Her use of some of the letters from her own name suggested that she was aware that there was a difference between experimental or play writing, and writing that everyone could read. Through seeing her name written at home and at school she knew that its written letter-shapes meant the same thing to others as to herself; the teacher also observed that, of the two ways of writing her name, Kerry had chosen her mother's use of capitals for the whole name, although she could recognize the school's upper and lower case version. The teacher was not concerned that this implied a rejection of the lower case letters; most of the signs on shops and hoardings in the local community were in capitals, and Kerry was used to picking out the letters of her name from them. It seemed likely that the capitals were simply the easiest point for this beginning writer to start.

From the observation the teacher learned important information about Kerry, and about children's understanding of literacy in the early years. Kerry knew that literacy is a process that is essential to our lives and that it embodies a public code; she understood that if she wished her lists to mean something to other people she would have to learn the publicly accepted letters to stand for spoken words. Kerry would be likely to enjoy helping to make shopping-lists or write messages at school, and she would like to have examples of 'real' words around her in the nursery. These words would carry important messages which people need to read, such as 'Please don't feed the fish – Kerry and Shaun are feeding them this week'.

From observations and assessments like these, we now understand much more about the way that experiences of literacy in the home and local community form children's notions of its uses, and how we can help children to extend their skills in reading and writing through building on their insights from home. Making a list before going to shop for materials for cooking at school springs naturally from children's home experiences, and from this children can progress easily to play with classroom shops and cafés, reading the names of foods they particularly like well in advance of any formal introduction to reading and writing. If parents can share in the play, the real shopping and the real cooking at school and at home, the children's learning is immeasurably enriched and stimulated.

THE SEARCH FOR BETTER TEACHING STRATEGIES

But this is only a beginning; there is much more to discover about how to teach effectively. The process of learning about children's growing understanding of the world has to be founded upon such apparently slight observations as that of Kerry's shopping list. It is the purpose of this chapter and the next to show how connections can be made between observation and assessment of children, and how what we learn in this way not only enables us to provide better for individual children's learning but also to make our ideas about the curriculum more closely matched to children's learning needs in general. The only way to make critical judgements about what we offer to children is through evaluating classroom provision. The only place to learn about what effective teaching is really like is in the classroom, through repeated observation and assessment of children.

THE 'EXTENDED PROFESSIONAL'

Pollard and Tann (1987) describe the potential of the teacher's role as that of the 'extended professional', who is able to link classroom practice and educational theory (p. xi). This role is crucial to quality in teaching, because it provides the theoretical framework within which teachers are not involved merely in 'reflective teaching', as Pollard and Tann describe it. They are also in a position to generate education theory in a more reliable way than ever before, by relating its generation to classroom realities. In an age which would call itself scientific, it is an extraordinary fact that education is as dominated by myth and superstition as was medicine before the Renaissance. The low status of teachers may have something to do with this, in that unlike doctors they have not been prone to think of themselves as likely to be the source of new learning and knowledge about an important part of human life and development. There may also have been an unwillingness to see young children as the fit subject of study – their role is too often seen as being that of humble students following the adults who have gone before.

Interest in young children in classrooms has been inspired by noneducational, and indeed non-human, studies. The coming of a renewed interest in animal behaviour has sparked off new ways of looking at children's behaviour in different settings (see, for instance, Smith's review of approaches in Pellegrini, 1988). The work of Bruner (1980) might have sparked off efforts by teachers to examine their own classrooms. Yet the essential investigative work of practitioners in developing insights to stand beside the work of professional researchers is largely absent, and is certainly not publicly acknowledged as a normal part of the work of the early childhood practitioner.

And yet, how else can educational decisions be taken, except on the grounds of what experience of children in classrooms has shown?

CURRICULUM DECISIONS IN NURSERY EDUCATION

In nursery education, curriculum decisions depend on the practitioner's assessment of children. Any discussion of nursery education must focus directly on the way that the curriculum is continuously developed in response to the learner. Assessment is an integral part of nursery education and informs all the educational decisions that are made. It is natural to see assessment as being an integral part of curriculum development, and to see the whole process as being founded on scrupulous observation of the children's behaviour and learning.

The work of the nursery practitioner

Children of nursery age come to school with a great deal of learning already established, and methods of teaching aim to build on this learning. In order to know how to build on this foundation teachers have to find out about children's interests and ideas, abilities and experiences, families and friendships. What parents have to contribute is of great importance – the home and local community are where children spend the majority of their time, and the influence of parents is in many ways greater than that of school. Practitioners must liaise with parents and others who know the children out of school if they are to gain a clearer picture of each child as an individual. They must observe how children behave in the classroom and the playground, on the way into the classroom and as they go home.

Children tell us about themselves through their behaviour, and there are clues to how we can best teach them to be found in their play and social interactions, in their conversations and the things they bring to school, in the way they use opportunities to explore new areas of learning and in the way they create stories, pictures, models and music.

The nursery team

The nursery team at its best is unique in its capacity to blend the insights of people with very different perspectives. The contribution of parents to the assessment of their children has a unique value. There are also notable differences in training which will give nursery teachers and nursery nurses a range of contexts for their judgements, while the needs of the children remain constant. The combination of these different perspectives gives assessment greater reliability. Within the team, one of the central aspects to notice is the kind of qualitative difference implied by the comparative depth of education for nursery teaching. The implications of this for leadership by teachers follow logically from this difference. The report of the Rumbold Committee makes this very clear in its final paragraph:

The complementary nature of the roles of those involved requires appropriately differentiated training which will not seek to impart the skills outlined above [in the report] to all in the same measure. The fact that many teachers of the under-fives will have undertaken a course of training lasting for four years and leading to honours graduate status should mean that they are able to take a lead in determining the quality, range and appropriateness of curriculum experiences for 3- to 8-year-olds, particularly but not solely within the school setting. Other roles will require other skills, and workers at all levels will have their own important parts to play.

(DES, 1990b, p. 47)

What seems most important to discuss is how assessment of under-fives can proceed in the absence of trained nursery teachers to guide other staff both in this and in the development of a high-quality curriculum which should follow the assessment. The Rumbold Committee were faced with an impossible task. They were committed to quality of educational experience for all under-fives, yet they were not given the means to make this possible. Quality of educational experience for each child depends on the way in which assessment informs the curriculum. Many people working in the field are aware of how much this process depends on a small number of professionals who have been trained for it. Not to have the freedom to make judgements about the inequalities in provision for the under-fives makes their brief a questionable one – you can have anything you want for the under-fives as long as it's what we've got already.

If teachers have these essential educational skills – and the Committee's report makes it plain in the last paragraphs that they believe that they do – how can it be right that so many under-fives do not have access to them? Only 24 per cent of three- and four-year-olds attend nursery schools or classes (DES, 1990b, p. 2), and although the Education Act 1980 empowers local education authorities to employ teachers in day nurseries this is seldom done (DES, 1990b, p. 3). The majority of under-fives are provided for by bodies and organizations which do not employ trained nursery teachers. This includes local education authorities who admit children under five to reception classes in infant schools.

The professional insights and range of experience of the Committee enabled them to draw a broad picture of present provision, but there can be no solution to the dilemma of quality within this picture without confronting the issue of the need for trained nursery teachers to lead teams in their educational decision-making. The Committee comment: 'A wide range of bodies and organisations is likely to be concerned in the development of services for young children. We urge them to take into account, in developing their strategies, the important issues of quality which we address in this report' (DES, 1990b, p. 6). In addressing its observations to the 'educators' of the under-fives the report aims to unite many different kinds of workers. The important issues of quality, however, are not so easily dealt with, and it is in the areas of assessment and curriculum that the greatest difficulties lie. If the curriculum is to be a personal one that has meaning for each child, it must be developed from a personal assessment. A formalized or closed assessment, perhaps in the form of a checklist, could not do the job, yet a personalized assessment demands a detailed and deep knowledge of child development combined with experience in observation and analysis. These educational decisions require a teacher who has been trained and educated to understand what is involved and who is working closely with the child at the time of the decisions.

THE PROCESS OF MAKING EDUCATIONAL DECISIONS IN NURSERY EDUCATION

In nursery education effective teaching is about making decisions on ways to follow up and extend the pupil's existing knowledge and understanding. In order to build on the foundations of each pupil's learning we have to be able to say what each pupil has achieved and what it would be appropriate for us to lead on to next.

Teaching, if it is to be effective, must be targeted at the learner's educational needs and stage of understanding. In order to target teaching appropriately, teachers have to use a range of methods of assessing children's progress, relevant experiences and interests, all of which will give helpful information about how to extend their learning.

The choice that is made among the different methods of assessment should reflect the principles of nursery and early years practice. These methods will be examined in detail in the next chapter; here, we draw attention to the connections between different kinds of assessment and the principles that underlie the education of very young children. These connections are capable of interpretation in the light of each child's development, whereas curriculum objectives and closed assessments are not.

Translating principles into assessment practice

The outstanding characteristic that early years education gives to assessment is its positive nature. The strengths, interests and experiences of young children are identified as the leading points for learning. Assessment is seen as providing a guide to further learning on the foundation of what has already been achieved, rather than as a narrow gate through which not all can pass.

Athey (1990) discusses the theoretical framework for this positive or, as she puts it, 'prospective' view of young children. She notes that Susan Isaacs developed this as distinct from the deficit view of cognition which came about from the particular research method that Piaget had used with children between two and five.

> Susan Isaacs and Piaget had great respect for each other. They visited each other's schools and were creatively critical of each other's ideas. Although they both observed young children closely, they drew different conclusions on early cognitive competence as they adopted different viewing positions. Put briefly, when assessment is carried out from a 'top-down' point of view, negative conclusions arise because younger children were seen as less competent than older children.
>
> A 'bottom-up' perspective, that taken by Isaacs, is founded on initial positive descriptions of cognitive competence in young children. When the more advanced thinking of older children is analysed, cognitive advances are apparent but do not detract from earlier competence.
>
> (Athey, 1990, p. 17)

Although the present discussion is set within the context of nursery education, the essential difference outlined here applies more widely. Its importance is in relation to its capacity to describe the strengths of individuals. This gives a far more accurate picture of the person as a whole than would a description of what were seen as weaknesses. If we want assessment to be a useful guide to a person's learning needs, we will have to look for the strengths in order to see what qualities are there to learn with – pupils do not make progress through what they cannot do, but through extending what they can already do to include what they cannot yet do.

Children are active learners; they build up their understanding of the world through constructing what one might call mental models of the world. It is essential for teachers to come to an understanding of the kind of model the child is using in order both to assess the level of understanding and to know what to offer next. Checklists, and closed assessments of all kinds, can link only with a closed type of curriculum, in which the child is forced to concentrate on what has not been achieved. They open up an easy avenue to the 'aims and objectives' type of curriculum, in which it is the adult's purposes which determine the child's activities, and in which those purposes are focused upon what has not been learned by the child. There is a grave danger of this turning into an ever-tightening downward spiral in which option after option is closed off to the child and to the teacher. In a classroom organized on these lines, the child who is most in need of help gets the least chance of it, because other things are seen as needing to come first. For instance, a child was excluded from the play activities which would have deepened his mathematical understanding because he had not satisfactorily completed an exercise in his book.

As a guide to providing for the individual learner this kind of assessment is needed throughout the early years of education. Its principles enable the teacher to see what a personalized curriculum might be like, and how this concept can be applied to provision for the group as a whole.

Essential principles of nursery assessment

Nursery practitioners and early years educators need methods of assessment which focus on the special characteristics of young children and on the activities young children engage in spontaneously. The assessment methods used need to capture the spirit and quality of early childhood, and should not be concerned primarily with skills and knowledge which are considered important at a later stage. For example, teachers of four-year-olds will want to record a whole range of skills, interests, knowledge and attitudes when observing children at play. They will not set out to assess and record only achievement within the National Curriculum attainment targets but will of course note evidence of this kind of achievement as part of the broader record.

Assessment of young children must cover all aspects of a child's development and must be concerned with attitudes, feelings, social and physical characteristics. These areas of development are interrelated and links need to be made between them. For instance, the child with a mild hearing loss may well seem immature socially and may have difficulty carrying out instructions.

Learning is not compartmentalized under subject headings for young children. When engaged in a cooking activity the children may gain experience of English (when discussing the processes involved or consulting the recipe), maths (when counting out spoonfuls, comparing sizes, weights etc.), science (when observing changes or dissolving substances), design and technology (when observing the effects certain tools such as a whisk have on the ingredients), history (when discussing how cake mixture was beaten before we had whisks), geography (when discussing which part of the world certain recipes come from and finding these on a map), personal and social development (when learning about the hygiene aspects of food preparation, and about which foods are most and least healthy), music (when comparing or imitating vocally sounds made by different utensils), physical education (when learning to control whisks, knives, cutters etc.) and art (when discussing patterns made by different implements, or decorating cakes or biscuits). Teachers need to observe and assess aspects of learning in all areas of the curriculum within the framework of one activity – they cannot set out just to assess mathematical learning since to do so would be to miss the wealth of other learning taking place. Any assessment tasks need to provide opportunities for children to demonstrate achievement across the whole curriculum.

Young children learn best from activities they have been motivated to choose for themselves. When assessing young children's learning it is important that we do not place them in situations which are unfamiliar to them and which do not motivate them. Young children's learning is context dependent and it is important that we recognize the impact which an unfamiliar setting has on achievement. We gain a much clearer view of what children know and can do when we observe them setting their own challenges and taking responsibility for their own learning. Parents have a role to play here in that they have a wealth of knowledge about their child's achievements and interests within the familiar and secure home and community settings.

One of the central aims of nursery education is to provide an environment where children can develop as autonomous, self-disciplined learners. Assessment procedures need to reflect this aim and should not place the child in a dependent situation where he or she is expected to carry out an adult-determined, adult-directed task. If tasks need to be set specifically for the purposes of assessment then they should take the form of a challenge which the child can pursue in his or her own way. At this stage of learning the process involved is more important than any end result and the child's creativity, persistence, resourcefulness and problem-solving ability are more significant than the application of existing knowledge and skills.

Young children learn best through first-hand experience – it therefore follows that they will demonstrate their achievement best through first-hand experience. Pressure to perform in test situations is not appropriate at this stage – such tests as the Goodenough 'Draw a man' test may seem simple to administer and to 'mark' but give an unreliable indication of a child's true ability, since to the very young child (and to older ones as well) it is the reason for doing something that determines the standard to which one does it. The process in which the child is engaged has to be understood as an integral part of the assessment. Drawing a man because one is asked to is very different from drawing one's elder sister Sharon got up to go out.

In the latter case, the eyebrows and eyelashes are essential since they are clearly of great importance to Sharon. To grade a child down for not drawing them in different circumstances is to show the inherent weakness of assessment in artificial situations.

Nursery practitioners and early years educators in general believe that the starting point in young children's learning is what they can do – not what they cannot. Assessment procedures should therefore set out to determine what each child can do, in order that provision can be made for each child's learning to be extended from that starting point. Too often teachers assess for failure and have a deficit model as a starting point for teaching.

Linking with the previous points it is clear that children's true potential will be demonstrated only if the context and ethos are favourable. If a child is set an unfamiliar task, which does not enable him or her to draw on previous *successful* experience, in an unfamiliar setting or context he or she is unlikely to be able to do himself or herself justice. The less experience of life children have the more unhelpful it is to place them in a 'no-win' situation of this kind. Instead teachers need to ensure that they observe and assess children in those situations where they are most likely to be able to demonstrate their full ability.

Children's learning and achievement are also affected by the relationships they have formed with their peers and with adults. These relationships can either enhance their self-esteem and thereby their learning, or destroy their confidence and undermine their ability to learn. These interpersonal factors cannot be ignored when assessing young children.

Assessment procedures are very influential. They differ widely in their starting points, and often lead in opposite directions from one another. From the study of them one can draw out the curricular implications and become aware how different the underlying assumptions are. As Athey (1990) has pointed out, these can be sharply opposed, although often certain curricular assumptions are taken for granted as if they were fixed in advance. Kelly (1990) shows how certain unexamined curricular assumptions underlie the National Curriculum, principally that the curriculum is made up of things that are to be learned about subjects, and how other models exist but are not discussed. Eisner (1982) and Egan (1988) relate principles of human learning and expression to the curriculum, in the same way as principles of human learning are related to the nursery curriculum. They show how a more appropriate curriculum can be developed in the light of what is learned from and with pupils at later stages of education as well.

NURSERY ASSESSMENT AND SUMMATIVE ASSESSMENT

Positive enquiry – what we can discover about children's existing understanding and strategies for learning – makes nursery assessment distinctive; the other main approach to assessment, the summative approach, 'places' the learner in the context of what might be expected to be the full range of possible achievement at this stage. It looks for what the learner cannot do as well as what he or she can do. This is the intention behind summative assessment – to seek the areas where the curriculum 'delivery' has not been effective. There are times at which summative assessment has a definite place but – particularly for very young children – the danger is that the way in which what should be achieved is articulated and itemized leads to a focus upon what the learner has not achieved. The arguments against this have been rehearsed above (pp. 53–5).

It might be asked whether there is a place for a summative assessment of children leaving nursery classrooms. This is a dilemma for nursery practitioners. On the one hand, they would like to share their knowledge with infant staff and to help children to settle down as quickly as possible. On the other hand, there is much against describing a child in terms of what he or she cannot do in one particular situation with one particular group of adults and children. The final point against a summative assessment at this stage must be that it is illogical to define in negative terms a child at its time of fastest development. It must be more accurate to say what the learner is able to do and understand, and to indicate the areas that are of most interest to the child. This kind of assessment enables the infant teacher as well as the nursery team to build up a different sort of picture of children as they enter infant education. It also gives them the information needed to move on to the next stage – the provision of an infant curriculum which can take the learner's achievements further through opportunities for new learning.

The stress implied in attempts to seek a 'baseline' assessment at five shows how the pressure for standard assessment at seven reaches down the age-range. Infant teachers, who are well aware that seven-year-olds are developmentally unsuited to standard assessment, are anxious that they will be held responsible for children's 'failure'. Reception teachers are under pressure to 'prepare' children for assessment at seven, and nursery practitioners are challenged to identify the 'areas of weakness' in order to show what their colleagues inherit from the nursery. It all sounds less and less like individual children going to school, and more and more like administrative buck-passing. At least in the nursery, practitioners must be prepared to stand up for the developmental needs of their children and for quality in assessment.

Putting the individual learner's needs first

There is another way in which assessment in the nursery takes a very different approach from that which seeks to standardize achievement. Nursery assessment takes its standards from the person being assessed, and only compares one child with others to establish very broad understandings. A child may not have had opportunities for vigorous physical activity outdoors, which would affect the way he or she made use of the playground opportunities. Another may not have been used to the enjoyment of a shared story, and without knowing this the teacher would be at risk of judging him or her to be uninterested in books. What is important is to see what progress is being made from the individual point of view and to try to understand what may be factors affecting the child for better or for worse. Standard tests cannot answer the most important questions, in that they cannot help us to see what meaning a child puts on the situation. Richard, aged three years seven months, could find another red object when shown one, and could repeat the word 'red'. Aged three years eight months he could not answer the question 'What colour is this?' when shown a red object. Instead, he beamed at his teacher and repeated, very softly, 'Colour'. The first test established that he could discriminate between colours, that he could make an appropriate choice, and that he could repeat a sound. What did the second test establish? That he had forgotten the word 'red'? That he had never understood the connection between the word and the colour? That he did not see any point in this dry and theoretical activity but that he enjoyed the social contact? As an attempt to standardize Richard's level of achievement, this test left too much unanswered.

Again, why 'test' children on such things as colours? Is it perhaps because it is easier for adults to do that than to try to see what mental activity Richard is engaging in? If so, this is very short-sighted, since there is plenty of other evidence available in the classroom. What perhaps is a difficulty is finding the mental adaptability and the professional self-confidence to use genuine, observed information in order to make assessments.

We need to find ways to ask the right questions. Richard's enjoyment of the social situation would be a good starting point, from which adults could explore further what he liked to do. It would be impossible to say that he was a child who had been assessed until his behaviour had been seen in the wholeness which he gave to it. Since assessment, as we see it here, is a positive process of identifying children's strengths, Richard's social interaction with adults should be examined as a process in itself. How would he respond to adult response? Could he take part in a game of repeating sounds? What kind of sounds might he respond to?

Special needs assessments, as much as any others, need to be on the child's own terms. Feedback is a natural part of assessment, as it is of human social relationships. Objectivity does not demand that the child is starved of response, any more than it demands that the assessment is withheld from the parent. Assessment that is personalized has an element of empowering the child in it, because of the support it gives to what the child can do. Much more of the 'testing' shown above, and Richard would be 'failed' at everything he did. Further investigation of what he could do would give a clearer picture and encourage him to be autonomous, too.

CAN WE RECONCILE THE TWO KINDS OF ASSESSMENT?

There can be no doubt that there are problems in this assertion of principles of assessment for those who look for ways to ensure an even 'delivery' of education to each child. It is not possible, with the kind of assessment discussed here, to extract information which will show whether certain content has been added to a child's mind, rather as particular features are added to cars on the assembly line. Nursery practitioners would say, however, that this is not a helpful way to view assessment. If the point of it is to see what progress a pupil is making, then it is more sensible to see how far, and in what directions, the pupil has travelled from where he or she was when last seen, than to pretend that everyone is travelling from the same point of beginning to another shared point of ending. The only context in which that can be a valid way of assessing human beings is if education is seen as training in a few basic processes and facts which will be common to everyone, rather as people are drilled in safety procedures. Even these procedures carry with them the underlying assumption that, if they fail, a creative adaptation or innovation is hoped for. Underneath the reliance on drill, therefore, there is an understanding that what is underpinning it is the capacity of humans to solve problems in new ways if the old ways are no good. These adaptations can be recorded, but by open, not closed, assessment.

The emphasis on each child's personal adaptation to the educational environment gives nursery assessment its creative and innovative quality. Nursery education is capable of responding to the needs of the age group in a way which places the development of each child in the central position. It has a wider relevance as well. If what has been said above is true for human learning at the nursery stage, surely it must be true for learning at later stages as well? It would be wise to be prepared to assess adaptability as humans become older.

EVALUATING THE CURRICULUM

It is understood that teachers at all stages will want to ensure that their curricular provision is giving each learner educational experiences across a wide enough range and to a standard which challenges and extends them. This evaluative function can also be best performed when evaluation is based upon the progress of the particular learners involved.

The process is the same as for assessment. Observation of children is the foundation of both, and practitioners can reflect on what is learned in the light of what they had originally planned.

The effectiveness of the evaluation lies in the way in which the information gathered through observation and record-keeping is analysed and compared with what the team originally planned. The educational provision is evaluated by being related to the children's development and learning as it is seen in their behaviour. This information enables the team to think how to make what they plan and do closer to the child's learning, and the conclusions are used to develop a curriculum that will take the child's learning further. The team plans for the arrangement of the learning environment and for the work of individual members of staff on the basis of this information.

Evaluating educational provision in this way – by reference to how it seems to meet the children's learning needs and interests – is quite controversial. It places the values and principles of nursery education in a higher position than conformity to prescribed targets of achievement. The implications of this are important. If in nursery education we dare to trust ourselves and the children this much, what does this say about the potential for professional self-development of teachers in later age-phases?

ASSESSMENT'S FOUNDATION IN OBSERVATION

From this brief account we see that the nursery curriculum is negotiated through assessment which is based on the careful observation of children. We now look at the ways in which observation provides the necessary data for reliable assessment of children.

The only way to gather evidence about how children are progressing is to observe their behaviour across different settings – in groups, as individuals, at play, in conversation, in structured teaching situations, with adults, and so on.

Fact-finding – the need for more accurate information

Observation is a normal part of the nursery practitioner's work. It may take the form of targeted observation, when practitioners withdraw from the pupils in order to focus on a particular child or situation. On the other hand, practitioners gather a great deal of information while they are at work with children. The latter is often described as 'participant observation' to make clear that it does not involve one in withdrawing from interaction with the class. Relevant items of information are noted in the course of classroom work and jotted down at the first opportunity. These notes form the basis for assessment and planning for individuals and groups, and are carefully written into class plans and assessments of particular children. This process will be examined at greater length in the next chapter.

An example of participant observation

Children are in the playground, watering plants. Some get trowels and explore how the water trickles onto the dry earth, forming puddles in the dust. The nursery nurse turns over a clod of earth to show that it is still dry underneath, and asks the children to fetch more water. Kerry says 'My sponge floats in the bath, and then I push it under'. They talk about how the water is 'floating' on the earth. The children would need more opportunities to understand why this happens, but they have observed the phenomenon. Kerry has interpreted it according to her previous experience. She has noticed that the water lies on top of the dry earth in the same way that a dry sponge lies on top of the bathwater. She can see the similarities; it will be the task of her nursery practitioners to help her to see that there are also differences. Further experiences with powder paint, flour and other dry substances are planned. Later on, there may also be experiments with oil on water. From this initial conversation and from others later, staff can see what children understand about the way different objects behave in relation to water.

Targeted observations

These will be discussed more fully in the next chapter. The point of using them is to discover more about a specific area. Richard's social relationships, play and conversation could have been studied in this way. Guidelines for structuring the observation and for analysing what is learned are outlined below (pp. 82–91). Criteria for further use will arise from the observations; Kerry's literacy understandings, once analysed, would give criteria for examining the curricular provision offered, for instance (see pp. 64–5, below). Some important issues in this process are now focused on.

WHAT DOES THE INFORMATION MEAN?

We must be aware that there are many points at which we, the adults, are the ones in the learning situation. There is no point in our undertaking observations in order to assess children if we do not learn from the information that we gather. Yet this is a difficult thing to do. Observations are not undertaken in order to reinforce or justify existing opinions, but to challenge and modify them. If this is to happen, we need a procedure that is as objective as possible.

The problem of objectivity

We would all agree that it is essential to make our judgements of children as objective as possible. This is the motivation behind the attempt to standardize assessment. This chapter has tried to make the case for believing that standard assessments do not give the most accurate or helpful information about children. It is now time to show how it is that observation-based assessment can be reliable. We must remember the principle that the criteria for making judgements should generally arise from the observations and the previous knowledge we have of the children.

The following chapter examines in detail how the nursery team can ensure that assessments are as objective as possible. There are two aspects that are important – the fact that more than one person, practitioner or parent, is involved in the assessment, and the way in which evidence is gathered very widely. As with Kerry's shopping-list, the child's writing and drawing, play and conversation, are all relevant, and provide a variety of perspectives.

DILEMMAS FACING NURSERY PRACTITIONERS

Can there be too great a contrast between the specific focus of individual observations and the general educational purpose of the practitioner? This is a genuine issue; how can an observation such as that of Kerry be useful for the development of provision for all the group? Observations of individual children are, in fact, valid as justification for overall classroom provision when they are looked at in the light of broad principles of learning. Kerry learned about the importance of literacy from observation of her mother; in this, Kerry tells us something about how all children learn, not just about herself. Kerry's use of the letters of her name tells us something about how all children acquire understanding of the symbolic meaning of letter shapes, and we can extend our understanding of this process to include other words that are familiar and meaningful to children.

It seems as if there is less of a dilemma here from the pedagogic point of view than from the political perspective, for if the practitioner is at ease with the idea that the curriculum can be evolved through observation and assessment of children, then it is hard to justify the imposition of curriculum from non-educational sources. There is a conflict between the practitioner as facilitator of the learning that children are embarked upon, and the practitioner as deliverer of a required curriculum. Although this is not often articulated directly by practitioners, the conflict of aims does have an insidious effect on their attitude to their work which undermines professional confidence.

EVALUATION AND SELF-ESTEEM

Practitioners in education are under great pressure from external agencies which profess to know 'what is wrong with teaching'. Where the debate on the teaching of reading is couched, even among the most respectable newspapers, in such terms as 'Inadequate lessons deplored by Clarke' (*The Times*, 10.1.91), teachers need to look to their own professional expertise for criteria by which to judge their performance. It is a hard thing to do in the absence of external support, but in the long run the only source of respect for teachers' professionalism is their own self-esteem. Teachers tend to be self-critical, because they work in a sphere where the responsibilities are great and the task unending. This critical tendency needs to be harnessed to the process of self-evaluation. Professional self-evaluation is essential to help develop the justified professional self-confidence which enables teachers to make informed responses to children and to check continuously how well they are meeting the needs of their children. Assessment is the key to this process, if we will give sufficient importance to the evidence we gather about the children's needs. If, in Kerry's classroom, a set of templates of letters for tracing lies on a table and she comes, with other children, to trace the letter that begins her name and then drifts off to take her baby to the shops, our assessment of her learning needs indicates that we should put our energies into providing imaginative play opportunities in which literacy has a natural place, and get rid of the tracing equipment. If we later see that Kerry and her friends are using the play resources to make an 'office' in which busy people leave messages copied from the telephone directory which they have signed with their own names copied from the labels under their coathooks, we can see that the classroom is supporting the children's learning. This is the kind of confirmation of professionalism that can justifiably build up self-esteem in teachers.

CURRICULAR IDEAS IN CONFLICT: THE FOUR-YEAR-OLDS

The contrast between the experience of four-year-olds in reception and in nursery classrooms is great (Ghaye and Pascal, 1988; Stevenson, 1988). All the good intentions of early years teachers in the infant school – and as we see from Pascal (1990) many reception teachers are not even infant trained – do not protect them from the influences on the infant curriculum.

The five-year-olds in the reception class come within the remit of the National Curriculum. National Curriculum assessment determines the structure of provision for them; the four-year-olds who share their experiences are also involved through the classroom provisions. This can mean a totally different educational process, so that it is not just a difference of range or quantity of educational input but a qualitative difference which makes for a different kind of education. Bennett and Kell (1989) provide an instructive look at the reality of children's experiences in reception classes. The free movement and social priorities of the nursery classroom do not form part of this experience, in spite of educational arguments in favour of co-operation. 'There is virtually no real, co-operative group work happening in British classrooms . . . There is, on the other hand, a mass of evidence, particularly from the United States, which attests to the benefits of co-operative group work . . .' (op. cit. p. 87). In this setting, the four-year-old's social and emotional needs cannot be met, and the case studies cited show how behaviour is dominated by anxiety and uncertainty (op. cit. p. 93, for example.) The requirement to assess children's progress in particular ways dominates the educational setting, to the detriment of their learning.

Improving the provision for four-year-olds

Contrast the megastructure of adults with the microstructure of children. Providing the right structure for play is a critical area; if the adults see it as peripheral to learning, the children must also learn to marginalize it. This is particularly the case in infant classes where the age-ranges, staff ratios and pressure of the National Curriculum threaten play. Outdoor play – the foundation of nursery provision for physical development, imaginative play, linguistic and social development, explorations of the natural world – disappears and is replaced by 'playtime'. Play in the classroom is under greater pressure even than before and at best is likely to find a justification in 'relaxation' or 'letting off steam' – a self-fulfilling description if ever there was one.

Social and emotional maturity is essential before concepts can be acquired – this too has implications for the assessment of under-fives. Children can be deskilled when these principles are not embodied in provision for them. The nursery curriculum recognizes the cognitive challenge of social relationships, just as nursery children find great satisfaction in them. Without the support of social relationships children may, as described by Bennett and Kell (1989), be unable to cope with the classroom at their normal level of competence.

There could be conflicts in the reception class between the need for child-initiated activities and the need to ensure a broad and balanced curriculum for the group as for the individual; the answers lie in the planning and awareness of progression in children's learning, and in understanding the impact of decisions taken about resources which could predetermine children's actions. Open-ended provision is very important. Of the two types of classroom – nursery and reception – the nursery pupils are much more effective and autonomous than those in reception classes. '. . . in too many primary schools much of the work is not sufficiently differentiated to match the span of ability and range of needs in mixed-age classes which include four-year-olds' (DES, 1989c, p. 33).

Experience in nursery schools and classes shows how the three- and four-year-olds work together within the group. Each has something to give and to receive. Four-year-olds gain in confidence because they are the ones who know how things are organized. They are at the top of their expertise, and assessment here reveals the strengths they can draw on.

A Turkish boy transferred from another institution to a nursery class. He had a reputation for being very difficult and for questioning and challenging staff in his previous institution, although he was also seen as being very quick to learn. Once established in the class he became a group leader quickly, because he was tall, strong and self-confident. As his confidence in himself and his surroundings grew, he began to take an interest in what happened and when. This enabled him to get the most from what was on offer, and it also gave him a purposeful relationship with others in the class. Gradually he began to make a role for himself as the helper of staff when children had to be organized. When it was time to come in from the playground, he began to make sure that the three-year-olds also came in when it was time, and from this he went on to pointing out to them when it was nearly time to come in as he observed the preparations for lunch. In this situation he could share the benefits of his grasp of class procedures; both he and the three-year-olds would have lost out if he had been plunged into provision for five-year-olds. Here, once again, he would have been unable to take an intelligent and co-operative part in the class proceedings, as in his first experiences. Whether or not he would have become again rebellious and challenging it is hard to tell. However, for the staff, the other nursery children, and the boy himself, an opportunity to see what he could do in appropriate surroundings would have been lost. This must be the ultimate description of the difference between positive and negative assessment, between seeing what children can do and what they cannot do.

Implications for nursery practitioners

Nursery practitioners need to take initiatives in re-educating society towards the principles of the nursery curriculum, particularly such aspects as the provision of play. Parents are always the most important audience and they can be reached at all points in their child's nursery education, from the 'pre-visits' onwards. Assessment of children's progress is the best source of justification for what teachers do. Assessment of each child gives parents the chance to see the role that play, and other aspects of the nursery curriculum, contribute to development.

The child development foundation of nursery practice is fundamental. Knowledge is needed to interpret observation and plan for a curriculum based on assessment. We must have time built in for observation, reflection and active curricular responses to the development of children's thinking about the world. For quality of assessment, practitioners need enough time, previous knowledge of the children, and suitable resources both material and human. Learning about children needs a foundation of understanding of child development in order to see the importance of what they do. Observation of outdoor play, for instance, is a rich source of information about children's thinking which is given a high priority in the context of nursery assessment. Without understanding its place in children's development and thinking, practitioners might see outdoor play as mere 'letting off steam'. In the next chapter we look in detail at how such insights are incorporated into assessment.

SUMMARY AND CONCLUSIONS

The quality of education depends upon the way in which assessment of children as learners informs the curriculum. Teachers are daily challenged to justify their actions and decisions to parents, colleagues and to the children themselves. They are also challenged by statements by politicians and opinions of the media. Without firm ground under their feet, how can they maintain the educational justification for what they do and say? If there is a place for debate about educational assessment it must be within the framework of the purposes delineated here. Systems of assessment which attempt to impose on education ideas developed in other contexts are not able to play the essential role of providing reliable justification for statements about children, for developments in curriculum, or for assertions about educational quality.

Teachers need confidence in themselves as professionals if they are to maintain education as an autonomous discipline; the quality of assessment is crucial to this.

4
ASSESSMENT IN NURSERY EDUCATION: A REVIEW OF APPROACHES

Margaret Lally and Victoria Hurst

As we saw in the previous chapter, staff working in nursery schools and classes have an in-built advantage when it comes to the assessment of young children – they always work in a multi-disciplinary team. Nursery teachers and nursery nurses have gained complementary knowledge and skills from their respective training courses, and consequently approach their work from different perspectives. Through discussing their perceptions of the children within their class they inevitably have to confront differences of opinion. These differences are often a direct result of the different emphasis in the training of teachers and of nursery nurses, but also reflect the personal values and attitudes of the individuals involved. Teachers of older children working alone with their class are less likely to face this challenge to their judgements, and some admit that they find team teaching situations threatening.

However, accountability demands that judgements made of children should be as objective as possible. Getting more than one perspective on the focus of attention is an important part of objectivity. This is why the nursery team approach is so valuable in assessment.

It is not just teachers and nursery nurses who communicate about the children in their class. Through close contact with parents and with others who have been involved with each child (such as child-minders, playgroup leaders, speech therapists, health visitors etc.) the nursery team broaden their view of children in their class. It is probably because of this collaborative approach to working with young children that approaches in nursery education have often been at the forefront of educational thinking about assessment.

THE DEVELOPMENT OF ASSESSMENT METHODS

As we have seen, nursery staff themselves are increasingly seeing assessment as an integral part of the curriculum development process. As their awareness of children's needs has been heightened by research evidence (outlined in the previous chapter) and their own experience, they have reviewed their practice and sought to find more effective ways of recording the experiences and achievements of the children in their group. Teachers attending courses reflect on the developments which have already taken place and those which are ongoing concerns. Many remember a time when very little was written down and much was 'kept in our heads'. Even at this time teachers talked about knowing the child as an individual, but there was less awareness of the dangers involved in allowing one person's view of the child to dominate.

As it was recognized that what is kept in the head becomes blurred, and even distorted or lost altogether, teachers began to realize the need to keep a written record. Initially this was kept mainly for children who were causing concern and who might need extra help. There are still teachers who see record-keeping in these terms – as an aid to providing evidence of 'problems'.

At this stage record-keeping in nursery education was usually based on checklists of the can/cannot do variety. Activities were set up to 'test' certain skills such as scissor control, turn-taking ability, colour recognition etc., and the 'results' ticked off for all children taking part. These checklists inevitably influenced the curriculum on offer, since if staff wanted to find out what a particular child could do they needed to make sure there would be an opportunity for skills to be demonstrated. The Keele Pre-School Assessment Guide (Tyler, 1979), which is one of the most sophisticated checklists in use in nursery education, clearly states that the information should be obtained through observation of children involved in the full range of activities, and that staff themselves should adapt the guide according to their needs and the characteristics of the children in their group. Nevertheless it is not uncommon to see nursery staff with children in a test style situation 'doing Keele'. The fact is that testing is less intellectually demanding of the adult than observing children and applying the information gained from observation to the items on the guide. Those teachers and nursery nurses who have been able to use the Keele guide in the way it was originally intended have done so creatively. They have questioned the usefulness of some items, added items of their own, and recognized the need for back-up information in the form of observations and work samples.

A major shift in attitude to assessment was caused by research evidence which demonstrated how schools were often failing children because they were not providing an environment which enabled each child to flourish (Wood, McMahon and Cranstoun, 1980; Tizard and Hughes, 1984; Wells, 1986). In fact some children were being considered by staff to be linguistically incompetent when research evidence demonstrated that they were quite competent in the meaningful contexts provided by their home.

In considering the implications of this research, nursery staff recognized the need to put the children at the centre of curriculum planning, rather than expecting children to fit in with a set of pre-defined demands made by the school. They realized that assessing children against a narrow range of skills, defined by the school and tested in contexts decided by the adults, would place many children at an immediate disadvantage – after all, school is an odd sort of place for young children and is in many ways quite different from the home environment they have become accustomed to. Instead of testing children against the skills schools value, it seemed more appropriate to find out about each child's previous experience, what they were interested in and what they had already achieved which could be built on within the nursery class. The aim of what Athey (1990, p. 17) describes as a 'bottom-up or "prospective" approach to assessment' was to make a better match between the child's interests and needs and the curriculum on offer in the nursery class. This approach is characterized by a positive view of children who come to school with a wealth of different knowledge and skills which must be valued and developed.

INFLUENCES ON THE DEVELOPMENT OF ASSESSMENT METHODS

This move away from adult-directed approaches to an approach which gives central importance to children's needs has presented nursery staff with some complex issues which they are still in the process of working through. These issues are worth outlining briefly at this point to demonstrate how assessment practice has been influenced.

The purposes of assessment

As methods of recording children's achievements have been considered, staff have had to ask themselves what their purposes are. Lally (1991, ch. 4) outlines six main reasons (identified by nursery teachers and nursery nurses) for keeping records:

1. To find out about children as individuals.
2. To monitor the progress (or lack of it) of individual children.
3. To inform curriculum planning.
4. To enable staff to evaluate the provision they make.
5. To provide a focus for communication with others.
6. To make the job more enjoyable.

This list is interesting because it focuses on more than the assessment of children. Nursery teams have also recognized the need to assess the provision they make and the way they involve themselves with the children. In other words, they recognize that they have an influence on the children's progress or lack of it.

Thinking about purposes

The purposes outlined above clearly require nursery staff to collect different kinds of information and to consider a range of methods for obtaining it. Clarity of purpose is essential if effective, useful methods are to be developed. Indeed, the dissatisfaction with checklists described above is a direct result of staff asking themselves 'What is the point of this? And of what use to us (and others) is this information?' Their answers to these questions led them to an understanding of the role of context in young children's learning – that, when they are highly motivated by challenges they have initiated for themselves, young children demonstrate skills, knowledge and attitudes which may not be evident at all in other less motivating contexts (Donaldson, 1978; Hughes, 1986).

For example, a child's drawing of herself will be considerably more complex if she draws alongside another child, and consciously aims to capture the differences between herself and her friend (by drawing details such as earrings, and patterns on clothes, and concentrating on facial features and hair style), than it would be if she was drawing herself in another context. What would a tick on a sheet tell anyone about this child's capabilities either at the time or later when the context has been forgotten? More seriously, how valid is it to ask a child to draw a person out of context for the purposes of 'baseline assessment'? Is it not more useful to look for the kinds of contexts which motivate the children to operate at their most sophisticated level? The answers to these questions will depend on our reasons for assessing – whether we wish to catch children out and find out what they cannot do, or whether we wish to record achievements as positively as possible.

It is somewhat ironic, therefore, that with the arrival of the National

Curriculum and the prospect of assessment at seven, attainment target-led checklists are being encouraged by some local authorities. Nursery staff, who have clarified for themselves the purposes of assessment and the consequent limitations of some methods, are in a strong position to take part in the debate. Nursery teachers are currently arguing strongly against the exclusive use of attainment target tick-lists, effectively exposing this method for the meaningless exercise it inevitably turns out to be.

Who can be involved in assessment?

A second issue which has been extensively discussed is concerned with involvement in assessment. An important principle in early childhood education is a concern for the whole child (Bruce, 1987; EYCG, 1989) not just the child we see in school. If we want to gain insight into a child's experience prior to admission to the nursery class, it is essential that key adults who have been (and/or are still) involved with the child are asked to contribute. It is increasingly common for nursery staff to involve parents in completing profiles of their child before admission to the class and in reviewing their child's progress during his time in the nursery (see Hazareesingh, Simms and Anderson, 1989 and Lally, 1991 for further details of these profiles). Nursery staff have also found it useful to talk with other workers who have known the child in different contexts (such as playgroup or toddler-club leaders, health visitors and speech therapists). In this way they gain a broader view of the child than they would if they merely observed him or her in the school situation.

The Primary Language Record (Barrs *et al.*, 1988) has encouraged those nursery staff using it to consider involving children in assessing their own achievements. This is consistent with the growing view that children should be encouraged to develop as autonomous learners with a valid viewpoint.

Involving a range of people in assessment sounds much more straightforward than it actually is. Involvement takes time and there is never enough. It also requires people to trust one another, and to listen to one another's views. Even within the world of education teachers complain that their colleagues do not take any notice of them – nursery teachers say that infant staff ignore their records and infant staff say the same about junior colleagues! Is it any wonder then that parents do not always feel that their views are properly valued?

However, perhaps the most vulnerable person in all of this is the child. If adults cannot take notice of one another what hope is there for the poor three- or four-year-olds struggling to make themselves heard? If we observe and listen to children we learn a great deal about their assessment of us and about the provision we make. If we actually ask their opinion about aspects of nursery life we are often surprised by the clarity of their judgements. Whether or not we are prepared to open ourselves to these judgements is another matter! After all, it is somewhat humiliating to be told by a four-year-old who has been invited to join in with the activity you have set up 'I don't want to do that. It's too boring'. Nursery staff, who have encouraged children to question and comment upon their nursery experience, have found that they have been forced to rethink and improve their practice to cater for the different interests and learning styles in their group. Instead of making the child who thinks an activity is boring join in, they concentrate on using their knowledge of children to present experiences in ways which motivate them. For example, children who by choice play outside on bikes and trucks can be inspired to use pens and paper through the setting up of a garage with a cashier's office.

If our reason for involving others in developing a fuller record of each child is to enable us to best meet each child's needs then we will be motivated to listen to and take account of all contributions. Staff who have established a collaborative approach to assessment talk in glowing terms about the ways in which this collaboration has affected their practice.

Adult expectations

Of course, the main strength of the collaborative approach is its ability to encourage individuals to balance their assessments against those of the others involved, and to identify the effects of their own expectations on their relationships with children. We know from research evidence (Tizard *et al.*, 1988) that adult expectations and interpretations of children's behaviour have a powerful influence on progress during the early years at school. Most nursery staff have heard themselves or others say something like 'Oh no, not . . . 's brother' as they glance down the admissions list. This is to some extent a very human reaction, but we need to be aware how that expressed or silent reaction to a child can influence our ability to respond positively to him. It can also influence our assessment of him in the school situation – in other words, we see what we expect to see, and the child acts as we expect him to act.

Parents can also hold negative views of their children, and nursery staff need to ensure that they do not reinforce these. Teamwork in nursery education encourages parents and staff to reassess their own perceptions and reactions in the light of the comments of others. It quickly becomes clear that one member of staff gets a more positive reaction from a child than another, and that the same behaviour may be interpreted differently by each member of the team.

The aim of the nursery teacher, who is the team leader, must be to encourage parents and staff to view each child positively – as an individual who has strengths as well as weaknesses. 'Teachers must believe that all children can flourish irrespective of initial IQ, of the effects of social class on entry to school and of future job opportunities' (Athey, 1990, p. 4).

Tackling inequality

From their knowledge of the children the team work together to create a learning environment which is appropriate to individual needs. They need to regularly ask themselves 'Does the environment we have created offer all children the chance of success or have we built in failure for some children?' One team reviewed story times because some children in their group were not developmentally mature enough to sit in a group to listen. They recognized that these children would at some point be able to listen in a group if they were given opportunities to look at books in a one-to-one situation with an adult. Making available to children what they currently need is the best way of ensuring they will reach the next stage, and yet it is all too easy to see children who do not conform to school routines as problematic. Nursery staff need to be aware that putting developmentally immature children, or those with special educational needs, into 'no-win' situations will disadvantage them further, and may also discourage them.

If we consider those children who find it most difficult to cope with school expectations, we begin to unravel some of the inequalities which need to be tackled. Children entering the nursery class come from a wide range of home and community backgrounds, and will be at varying stages of development. Some children will speak a language other than the language of the school, and even those whose first language is English may find school talk bewildering (the usage by teachers and nursery nurses of the phrase 'would you like to . . .' when no choice is intended – as in 'would you like to tidy up now?' – is a source of much frustration for young children who reply 'no'!). As far as assessment is concerned, staff need to ask themselves how the language they use puts some children at a disadvantage. It is only possible to gain insight into the knowledge and understanding of bilingual children if assessment is carried out in the child's first language. Where language support staff are available this can be achieved, but in many situations staff are aware that their assessments of some children are limited.

Similarly, the materials, including assessment materials, used in nursery classes may be culturally biased in favour of middle-class white children. If we wish to find out about the children's language it is clearly unfair to assess all children discussing the same picture or book – unless of course we want some children to do badly! Kim, a three-year-old Vietnamese child, was generally silent but was inspired by the introduction of the book *Mealtime with Lily* (ILEA, 1984) to make her first utterances in English. She was inspired because she strongly identified with the character Lily. If the staff wanted to assess her use of the English language, this was the book to use. After all, what would be the point of giving her a book which they knew would elicit no response? There would be no point at all, unless we are most interested in the assessment materials and a misguided concept of fairness rather than in the child's real ability.

Gender is also a potential source of inequality. Children arrive at nursery with stereotyped views of male and female roles. They may believe that they are not capable of tackling some activities because they are a girl or boy. This will obviously affect the curriculum choices they make and their achievement. Nursery staff have an important role to play in assessing attitudes – their own, the children's and the parents' – and in challenging stereotyped ideas.

Assessment methods

Earlier in this chapter we began to consider the ways in which assessment methods in nursery education have evolved. With the current interest in assessment it has never been more important for nursery staff to continue to test out their approaches against the principles of early childhood education (Bruce, 1987; EYCG, 1989). The process of translating principles into practice was explored in the previous chapter. Assessment in nursery education is developing to take account of the insight we have gained from this exercise. It has raised questions about some of the methods currently in use.

For example, if our aim is to encourage children's development as autonomous, independent, self-disciplined learners, is it valid to put them into assessment situations where they are dependent on an adult for direction? Similarly, if we believe that play, active exploration and talk are important features of the learning process for young children, is it valid to assess children only in passive, seat-based situations?

Perhaps most importantly we need to ask to what extent our methods challenge us. Are our methods closed – i.e. offering only one answer of the can/cannot variety – or are they open – i.e. allowing for children and/ or provision to surprise us? If we return to our purposes outlined earlier we see that methods must be developed which enable us to look as objectively as possible at the children, the provision and ourselves. If our methods are genuinely to influence our approach to individual children and to the curriculum we offer then they must tell us things we did not expect to find out. Assessment methods must challenge rather than reinforce our expectations, and must raise questions as well as provide answers.

Are our assessments useful?

We can see that there are no easy solutions. The education of young children is a complex undertaking. It is not about adults filling empty heads with knowledge which can be ticked off on a sheet. Those who believe it is this simple will devise equally simple assessment methods, and may delude themselves that they know about children. More enlightened nursery teachers have realized that complex processes require complex assessment methods. They are aware that they need to evaluate the methods they use against the purposes for assessment they have identified. With the purposes outlined earlier in this chapter in mind, we can see that for assessment methods to be useful they must:

- highlight each child's personal interests and achievements (nursery staff need to understand that these will not necessarily coincide with their own view of what children should be interested in or should be able to do);
- demonstrate whether a child has made progress or not in all areas of development – in the early years social, emotional and physical development are as important as intellectual development (ESAC, 1989);
- raise questions about the provision which has been made for the children and about the quality of adult interactions with particular children;
- give staff clues for developing the curriculum in such a way that it meets individual needs;
- facilitate communication with others who know the child or who will be working with the child in the future.

ASSESSMENT METHODS CURRENTLY IN USE IN NURSERY EDUCATION

Getting to know children as individuals is a worthy and important aim, but in reality presents staff with problems. Many children attend nursery class part-time and it is not uncommon for a teacher and nursery nurse to have to keep records for 50 children (25 attending in the mornings and 25 attending in the afternoons). Assessment methods currently in use have been developed to provide as much information as possible from a variety of sources. These methods include:

- forms to be filled in before admission to the nursery providing a profile of each child. This information is supplied by the child's parents and by others who have known the child. Interpreters may be used to support those parents whose first language is not English. Nursery staff value these profiles because they give insight into the child's home and community experience which can be built on in school, as well as providing important information about the child's needs (e.g. dietary requirements, behaviour management etc.); and parents value the fact that their intimate knowledge of their own child is recognized;
- written observations which provide a record of the child's experience in school, and information about the appropriateness of the learning environment;
- a collection of dated work samples (such as drawings, models, early writing, plus photographs of children engaged in other activities, and tape recordings of language and/or story telling) demonstrating significant stages in the child's development;
- checklists to record quickly aspects of nursery life such as use of the learning environment by adults and children or the involvement of adults with children. Checklists are also used to record developmental achievements but, as we saw earlier, their limitations have been recognized, and many teachers feel they are useful only if they are cross-referenced to observations, or if they have a space for comments where contextual information can be added;
- summaries of a child's achievements completed at regular intervals (e.g. termly) during the child's attendance at nursery. In completing these summaries teachers draw on information obtained from all the methods outlined above (an example of the kinds of information covered is to be found in Lally, 1991). They discuss the summary with their team and often with the child's parents (whose views may be added to provide a home-based perspective), highlighting the child's strengths and

weaknesses, and deciding what support is needed to ensure the child's continuing progress. A regular review of each child is essential if staff working in a busy nursery setting are to maintain their focus on individual needs. The record which is completed before children transfer to the reception class is an example of a summary of achievements but of course it is much too late from the nursery staff's point of view to focus on children just as they are about to leave!

It will always be the case that more information about children will be held in the heads of staff than will be written on paper. An important contribution to assessment methods in nursery education is made by informal discussions between members of staff and between staff and parents. These discussions which happen every day are one of the most enjoyable aspects of teamwork. Recalling the day's events and sharing them with others helps adults to take stock and make sense of what could otherwise seem like an unrelenting assault course! It is often during these discussions that different perspectives on the same events are put forward, or new information is remembered which helps the member of staff telling the story to see the incident in a different way. A wise teacher adds the main points of these informal discussions to the relevant child's records, or adjusts curriculum plans to take them into account.

OBSERVATION – THE KEY TO ASSESSMENT

The main tool for all the methods outlined above is observation. The quality of the observations and of the analysis of these observations will determine the quality of the assessments made. Stepping back for a few minutes and trying to tune into what is actually happening (as opposed to what we expect to see happening) by writing down what we see and hear is the only way to challenge our thinking. To some extent our observations will always be subjective, since we always bring certain assumptions and prejudices to our work, but observation (particularly if we discuss our findings with others) is the best chance we have of an objective approach.

Observation is usually an important feature of early years courses, but as Lally (1991) points out, some teachers and nursery nurses have not been taught the purpose of observation, and cannot see the need to continue to observe once they leave college. Discussions with nursery staff reveal that:

● some think they can keep observations in their heads and feel they have no time to write anything down;
● some only observe children they are worried about;

- some complete written observations but say they do not know how to make use of them.

However, many nursery teams have realized that observation has a vital role in informing all parts of their work and are developing more effective systems to ensure that all children and all areas of provision are focused on, and that at least some observations are carefully analysed. They have learnt that there must be a structure to their approach to observation. For example, one team discovered that they needed to ensure that their observations covered all areas of development (and not just particular skills), when they looked at one child's records and found that they had all focused their observations on social aspects of his development.

ORGANIZING FOR OBSERVATION

Making time to observe

If observation is a priority, time must be found for it. Many nursery staff would argue that they are engaged in observation all the time as they work with the children, and it is true that much nursery observation is of necessity of the participant variety. If staff make notes as they work with individual children or small groups, they provide themselves with a very valuable record, but it is not enough. If only participant observation is involved, it is inevitable that the picture built up will be a narrow one. Staff admit that there are some children and some areas within the learning environment that they spend less time with (or none at all). If they do not participate in these areas or with these children, they close themselves off from the possibility of observing the nursery class in its totality. Similarly, if they make notes about children only when they are involved with an adult, they miss out on the range of skills children demonstrate when they are playing alone or with their peers.

Two four-year-olds in one nursery class had spent the greater part of the morning making pyramids and cubes with interlocking plastic triangles and squares. Their language (including mathematical language) had been rich and fluent and they had worked very co-operatively together. At story time a member of staff asked them to show the other children what they had made, and encouraged the whole group to count the number of sides of a pyramid and the sides of a cube. The two children who had constructed the models showed no interest in this exercise, although they had demonstrated in their play that they knew how many sides were involved – as far as they were concerned they were being asked to state the obvious. Nursery staff must observe and assess children in child-initiated tasks as well as in adult-directed ones if they wish to gain a full picture. They must also observe the process and not confine their assessment to a discussion of an end product. The nursery nurse in the example could easily have underestimated the mathematical competence of these children.

Most nursery staff find time to make notes as they go along but find it harder to make time to stand back for a few minutes to focus on something they might otherwise miss. They also say they feel guilty about standing back and worry about what others might think if they are seen apparently doing nothing with the children.

This idea that nursery staff must always be 'busy' has been a most unhelpful one. It has led in some cases to a crisis-management style of working where staff respond to those happenings and children which draw most attention to themselves. With this style of operating, noisy children gain most attention at the expense of quieter children, and there is a risk that the behaviour which staff find least acceptable is actually rewarded. If staff make time for focused observation, and for reflecting on what they see and hear, they will become more aware of the reasons why things happen, and why children behave in the way they do, and will be more able to take preventative measures.

In order to be able to observe in a focused way, staff need to organize their nursery to enable children to operate as independently as possible. If equipment and resources are organized and labelled in such a way that children can select the materials they need to pursue their own interests and projects, and if they are encouraged to tidy up after themselves, nursery staff will be relieved of many of the chores associated with their work and will have more time to interact in depth with and observe the children. This seems obvious and yet nursery staff still busy themselves with supervisory tasks such as putting on aprons and getting things for children, and then complain that they never have any time. Some staff underestimate the abilities of children. If we are to encourage independence, we must have high expectations of young children and must understand that tasks, which are laborious chores to adults, are exciting learning experiences for three- and four-year-olds. If the environment is carefully and appropriately resourced, and support is given, most children cope well with and enjoy the responsibility they are offered.

While organization is important, it is also essential to increase the number of adults working with the children as often as possible if observation is to become a regular feature of nursery life. Students, parents and other carers can all offer valuable support to the teacher and nursery nurse and their involvement should be welcomed and planned for.

Above all, however, staff need to really believe that observation is important. The most committed teachers and nursery nurses manage to find plenty of time for observation. They *plan* to observe in the same way that they plan to work with a group of children, and they discover that the more they observe in a structured, focused way the more they see incidentally. Perhaps all nursery staff need to ask themselves whether, when they say they have no time, they are really saying they do not see the point of observation.

What should nursery staff observe?

We have already made it clear that nursery staff need to assess themselves as well as the children. One observation can provide information about the provision and the adult involvement in a situation as well as information about the child. However, staff need to have some idea of what it would be useful to focus on and need to see some purpose in observing, since without this they often get sidetracked and observation is forgotten.

These focuses and purposes should not be narrow ones. Observation should be approached in a genuine spirit of inquiry, with a strong desire to find out some answers to the real questions which are posed within the nursery situation. Nursery staff who regularly reflect on their work have no difficulty raising their own questions, and those teams who have drawn up guidelines for observation have often done so in the form of a series of questions.

These questions might be grouped under the following headings which highlight the three main areas of inquiry for nursery staff (in each section some indication of possible ways of approaching these questions is offered).

Observing children:

How are the new children settling into the nursery class?
In order to find some answers to this question it is necessary to observe each new child at different times of the day (e.g. parting from his or her parent/carer, at various points during the session in and out of doors, at group times, using the toilets etc.) to discover the response of these children to the new environment they find themselves in – how they spend their time, with whom, what they particularly enjoy, what worries them etc.

Discussions with parents are vital during the settling-in period, since children will reveal worries or enthusiasms to their parents, which they may not share with the nursery staff. Parents will also value some insight into their child's first weeks in school and sensitive staff share their observations so that the child may be supported by all adults involved with him or her.

How are individual children spending their time?
This is an important question, since, because most nursery staff encourage children to make choices, it is not always easy to build up a picture of how an individual spends his or her time. HMI (DES, 1989c) warn that there is a danger of a child's experience becoming fragmented unless adults plan to avoid this. Insight can be gained from time-sampling observations where a child would be observed at fifteen-minute or half-hourly intervals during a session (or better still several sessions). Each time the child is focused on notes are written to indicate where the child is, what he or she is doing and with whom. A scan of the nursery as a whole at the same time intervals, noting which children and which adults are in each area of the nursery, can also offer some insight into the ways in which children spend their time. If it is revealed that some children choose to spend most of their time at one activity or in one area of the nursery (such as the home corner or block area) staff may wish to find out, through more focused observation of the quality of the child's experience, whether this is because of insecurity and a fear of trying new things, which they could help the child with, or because of a deep interest which is developing and could be developed further. In this way staff are able to assess the needs of individuals and make plans to support and extend learning.

What kinds of relationships are the children developing?
As we explained in the previous chapter, it is always important to examine the relationships encouraged (either intentionally or unintentionally). Are aggressive children allowed to dominate certain areas of provision at the expense of more timid individuals? Do staff actively encourage children to co-operate and negotiate with one another? And so on. Social relationships are cognitively very demanding and nursery staff have a particular responsibility to support children with the social learning involved in coming to terms with being a member of a large group (Lally, 1991). Positive and negative aspects of the relationships in the class need to be identified (e.g. special friendships, children who are isolated, children who find it difficult to take turns or share etc.), so that the staff can take steps to encourage the kind of behaviour which respects the right of all children to equal access to the curriculum, and enhances each child's self-esteem.

Information gained from studying where children spend their time may shed some light on or raise some questions about relationships (e.g. Why is it always those three boys in the block area? Tammy and Andrew played together all session, and so on), but closer observation will be necessary to discover why a child seems to be unable to get involved with others, or why a child is behaving in a particular way. If all members of the team plan to focus on an individual over a week, identifying times of day when they particularly need to notice what is happening, and then share their observations, they invariably discover ways of supporting the child, and at the same time expose further questions which need to be asked. For instance, is the environment one which supports relationships? Is the curriculum one which encourages children to learn together? As far as relationships are concerned it is essential to look both at the group as a whole and at the individuals who make up the group and contribute to the way it functions. Because they have a vital role to play in the group, adults will find that, as a result of their investigations into children's behaviour and relationships, their own impact on the group is called into question.

What are the children's interests and what are their attitudes to learning and their feelings about being a member of the nursery class?
Through watching and listening carefully to children it is possible to gain insight into their interests, their levels of confidence and independence, their persistence at tasks and their feelings about being in the nursery and about the learning experiences on offer. Once again discussion with parents is vital to gain a fuller picture of the child. If, for example, the teacher has been told by a child's parents that they went to visit granny on a train at the weekend, she can ensure that resources are available for this child to pursue this interest should he or she choose to do so. Similarly, if it has been observed that a child regularly says 'I can't draw', parents and staff can work together to help him or her gain confidence in his or her own ability.

What knowledge, skills and understanding are children demonstrating when taking part in both adult- and child-initiated experiences?
The introduction of the National Curriculum has drawn attention (some would argue too much attention) to this area of assessment. Nursery staff have always recognized the need to find out what the children know and can do, and many are highly skilled at building a curriculum around this starting point. This is why they have been so successful in identifying and responding to children with special educational needs. Through observation, teachers and nursery nurses gain access to the children's knowledge

and understanding of the world around them, and to the skills they are able to use in the pursuit of their own challenges. It is essential to observe what children choose to do if we wish to develop a responsive curriculum for them. A regular review of knowledge and skills is necessary if we are to be sure that progress is being made, and that it will continue to be made. Dated work samples, photographs and tape recordings (of language and story telling) are useful here to back up observational evidence. The National Curriculum has encouraged a greater emphasis on subject-based assessment. This has not been a problem for those nursery staff who have always seen observation as the main assessment tool. They recognize that each observation provides evidence of learning across the curriculum as well as offering insight into the personal and social aspects of the child's experience. Lally (1991) explains how some nursery staff are developing ways of gaining access to evidence of subject knowledge, skills and understanding contained in observations so that they can pass on relevant information to the child's next teacher. Reception teachers need increasingly to take careful note of the evidence of learning provided by their nursery colleagues, if they are to encourage progression rather than regression.

Are all the children making progress in all the above areas of concern?
Regular reviews of children's total experience should reveal the extent to which children are continuing to make progress in all areas of development and should alert staff to children who are becoming bored and disruptive because they are not being stretched intellectually, or are unable to learn because of social and/or emotional difficulties. Close observation of these children should help staff identify their needs and make plans to help them.

Observing the provision:

How effectively have we organized space, time and resources?
All teachers have to contend with at least some limitations on space, time and resources. It is essential, however, that we do not allow these limitations to narrow our thinking and stop us from striving to organize what we have in the most effective way. We need to observe the space as a whole (in and out of doors), and specific areas within it, to discover whether the children are able to move freely between areas and whether they can play in groups of varying sizes without getting in one another's way. We need to ask which areas of provision are used most/least well and why this is the case, and we need to act in response to our findings (a possible framework for asking these questions through observation is offered in Drummond,

Lally and Pugh, 1989, section 8). We also need to consider the organization of resources and the extent to which children have been enabled to select and put away the equipment and materials they need – if it is discovered that there is confusion about some pieces of equipment when it comes to tidying-up time, work can be undertaken with the children to solve the problem. In one nursery, labelling shelves in the home corner with pictures and silhouettes of the equipment to be placed there, immediately stopped children from stuffing as much as possible into the cupboard – it also turned tidying-up into a fun activity.

Our organization of time also needs scrutiny if we are to discover whether the daily routine is in the best interests of the children. For example, if we observe what happens when children are not allowed to use the outside area for the first hour or half hour of the session, we see that when the door is opened there is a sudden rush of children out of the classroom (many of whom will be leaving activities they have not completed) and boys are usually at the front of the queue waiting to grab the bikes etc! This kind of organization encourages the outside provision to be seen mainly in physical terms rather than as an extension of the classroom where the whole curriculum can be offered. Another aspect of time which is being considered by nursery staff is story time. When is the best time for this and do all children need to be involved at the same time? Perhaps the central question that needs to be asked honestly in relation to all these organizational issues is: are we organizing in this way because it is best for the children, or because it is most convenient for the adults involved?

To what extent does our provision offer quality opportunities for cross-curricular learning?
Sadly an often neglected area of inquiry is the quality of the learning environment in terms of the resources on offer to the children. Tatty books and pieces of equipment remain in place long after they should have been repaired or dispensed with, and the effects of them on the children's attitudes are underestimated. If we want children to care about their environment and develop high standards then we must set the example. When assessing areas within the nursery we must ask whether the space and resources are attractively presented, whether new equipment needs to be offered to extend the children's experience and whether it is possible for children to gain experience across the curriculum in whichever area they have chosen to work in. The Early Years Curriculum Group (EYCG, 1989) demonstrates how well resourced areas such as the block area, the home corner and the outside area can offer experience within all subject areas.

However, if some outside areas or home corners are observed we can see that they are not offering quality of this kind. Nursery staff need to regularly observe the provision they have made (both when it is being used and after the children have gone home) to assess its potential as a rich learning environment. Some teams have drawn up guidelines setting the standard for each area (what it should look like, how it should be resourced etc.) against which they can regularly monitor its quality.

What are the children actually gaining from taking part in each activity?
This question particularly needs to be asked when observing adult-initiated activities. We need to be able to accept that as adults we often have a narrow view of learning, and that the activities we set up are often sterile and unimaginative compared to the activities set up by children for themselves. Compare, for example, a pattern-copying activity set up by an adult which involved a four-year-old child in copying a row of beads in repeating patterns, with the spontaneous experience of repeating patterns gained by a three-year-old who painted a row of stripes onto a triangular piece of paper making sure he got the colours in the right sequence. In the first example the adult did most of the thinking – it was her idea which the child copied with very little effort within two or three minutes. The three-year-old, on the other hand, had the idea, and executed it himself with no reference to anyone else, taking almost fifteen minutes to work through the process of getting the colours in the right order. It is useful to ask ourselves which child was demonstrating a greater understanding of repeating patterns, and would the three-year-old have been able to complete the adult-directed version of the task – and does this matter? A full assessment of children's ability must involve an assessment of the context they were working in at the time, including an assessment of the intellectual processes involved for the child.

Observing adults:

We have already indicated that adults must assess their own influence on children, through the provision they make and through their interactions with them. Of course it is difficult, if not impossible, to observe ourselves, and most adults feel threatened by the idea of someone else observing them. In a nursery class, however, we are always observed to some extent by other adults and, even when the focus is primarily on children, observations of adults are often involved. Whether we share our observations with one another will depend on the trust between staff members. If we really believe that the way we interact (or do not interact!) with children has an effect on them, and that the effect might not be a positive one, we would see that we need to adopt a braver approach towards mutual observation of team members. If we can be clear that the observer will not make judgements – that is, he or she will record as far as possible exactly what happens and what is said and give this to the other person without comment – some of the threat is taken away, since control over the observation and any analysis of it is given to the person observed. This is the only way we can really reflect on our own practice. Tape-recording or better still video-recording ourselves are other possibilities.

It is interesting that most adults are very reluctant to allow themselves to be observed in this way, revealing a fear of what they might find out. A more positive way of approaching our work would be to accept that we all have strengths and weaknesses, and that we can all improve the way we work with children. We cannot improve, though, if we are not aware of what we do well and what we do less well. In order to build trust within a team it might be useful to ask each member to make a list of the strengths (as far as working with the children are concerned) for all other members of the team, to give these lists to one another, and discuss them. (As part of this discussion, weaknesses within the team as a whole might be identified and the possible effects of these weaknesses on the class examined. In this way all staff would be able to see that they were valued by their team members and had quite definite strengths which were recognized.) It is only possible to look at weaknesses in ourselves if we are aware we also have positive characteristics.

When observing adults in the nursery class the following questions might be explored:

Where do we spend our time?
Adults give powerful messages to the children about the activities and children they value by spending more time with some activities and with some children and less time with others. If we are to ensure that all areas and all children have adult involvement we have to find out which areas and children are currently neglected, which receive too much attention and why this is the case. Simple time-sampling procedures (as described earlier) carried out over several weeks can provide this information, as can daily diaries kept by all staff in which they note where they involve themselves and with whom. Some teams note on plans their names and the names of children against the areas of experience they were involved with for a reasonably sustained length of time. They can then check at the end of each week what has been neglected.

How do we spend our time?

This question should lead to an investigation of the quality of interaction with children. Are adult–child interactions of a conversational, mutually supportive kind based on a notion of equality, or are they of the controlling, managing kind with adults taking the lead role and doing things for children and telling them what to do, or are they a mixture? Do the interactions between adults and children encourage the attitudes and behaviour the team wish to encourage? For example, if we want children to become self-disciplined, what is the effect of us telling children they cannot do something without explanation?

Which children and parents do we relate to most/least easily? Why?

The answers to these questions may reveal painful information about our values and attitudes. Are the families we relate to best those who are most like ourselves? If so, what messages do the other families get from us and what effect does this have on their progress through our class? One way of discovering our response to families is to observe parents and children coming into the nursery – which parents are most/least at ease? – and to note which parents and children we spend most and least time with. We also need to consider the quality of our interactions with individual children and parents. Are all our discussions with some families of a negative kind (e.g. to do with unacceptable behaviour etc.)? To what extent are we reinforcing certain behaviour through our approach? Are we enhancing or destroying a family's self-esteem? Unless nursery staff can discover why they respond in the way they do it is impossible for them to work towards more positive relationships with all families, and the inequalities with which some children enter school may be compounded. It is too simple to write some families off as being 'a problem' and to blame them. It is up to professional staff not to take the simple route but to expose themselves (their attitudes, beliefs and behaviour) to scrutiny. As we stated at the beginning of this chapter adults have a profound effect on children's progress through school. Our assessments of children must take this into account.

Analysing observations

Although it is useful and often essential to use questions as a starting point for focused observations, it is also possible and desirable to start sometimes from random or spontaneous observations and see what they can tell us. We have developed a framework for analysing observations of all kinds which should uncover answers to many of the questions raised above and incorporates planning and assessment (first used by Hurst and Lally at a conference led by EYCG at the National Children's Bureau in November 1989; see Figure 4.1).

This framework contains a further series of questions designed to encourage staff to:

- acknowledge their previous experience of the child and place the observation in the context of this knowledge;
- make use of their observation to inform their assessment record of the child;
- raise further questions about the child's experience – these may be in connection with the role of the provision, or of the involvement of children or adults with the child – in this way one observation can be seen to inspire further investigation;
- use the information they have gained to plan to support the child's future learning;
- communicate with one another as they share and analyse one another's observations.

Figure 4.1

Questions to provide a framework for analysing observations of the learning experiences of individual children.

1. What is the significance of this observation in your experience of this child (e.g. does it indicate progress, regression, the development of a new interest or skill, a change in attitude etc.)?

2. What does this observation tell you about this child's interests, experience, skills, attitudes and knowledge? How do these relate to the programmes of study/attainment targets of the National Curriculum? (You may wish to consider how you could record this information.)

3. What additional information would you like to collect to gain a clearer picture of this child (i.e. what questions about this child has the observation generated)? What have you learnt about the provision which is being made for this child?

4. How would you want to use the information you have collected through observation as a basis for planning to support and extend this child's learning? (This should include a consideration of the provision of equipment and experiences as well as possible adult involvement.) However, it is important to recognize that these plans must be flexible (i.e. respond to the child's developing interest) and not imposed on the child.

Margaret Lally and Victoria Hurst (1989)

We have encouraged teachers and nursery nurses to use this framework to analyse observations which they have brought along to courses and conferences. They have been surprised to discover that even a seemingly insignificant observation completed quickly for the course has revealed on analysis all kinds of unexpected information about children, the provision and adults. More detailed observations have been the source of a wealth of evidence.

It is not suggested that every observation could be analysed in such depth, but that some could be. Some staff have decided to focus on one or two children each week and use the framework to analyse their collective observations during their weekly meeting. In this way they are able to add to the children's assessment, and to use the information they have gained to plan ahead. This is an effective way of making observation and children central to curriculum development. These staff are discovering that taking part in a formal analysis exercise such as this sharpens their thinking and helps them to make better use of all observations. The questions are quickly internalized and applied spontaneously during their day-to-day work as they observe what is happening.

This is a rigorous process both for them and for the children, who quickly learn that they will be focused on in all kinds of ways, not just when they have behaved in an unacceptable way or when they are directly involved with an adult. Through the process of observation itself, and through the use they make of their observations, nursery staff indicate clearly to children what is expected of them. Classes where observation is a regular feature are demanding places for children – they know that unkind behaviour will be dealt with, that real achievement will be recognized, and above all that everyone will get some of the adults' positive time. It is in classes like this that *all* children are encouraged to reach their full potential, not just the children who conform most readily to school expectations.

SUMMARY AND CONCLUSIONS

Throughout this chapter the emphasis has been on assessment as a kind of detective work – finding clues and investigating more and more. Nursery staff, because they work with creatively unpredictable young children, are developing ever more sophisticated approaches and, as they do so, are recognizing that definitive statements about children are not possible. It is true to say the more answers you seek the more questions you raise!

This chapter has traced the development of assessment methods in nursery education, examined some of the issues which are influencing thinking, and explained why some methods are losing favour with skilled staff. The central role of observation has been emphasized and a framework for carrying out and analysing observations has been suggested. Throughout the chapter, the value of sharing perceptions with others (including the children themselves) has been stressed. A major aim of assessment must be to help us see things from the children's point of view.

Nursery staff have always been vulnerable to 'top-down' pressure and some have already been asked to complete assessment sheets which are in conflict with their beliefs. If it is recognized that nursery staff have been the pioneers as far as assessment is concerned, and have a great deal to offer their colleagues, then maybe a welcome result of the National Curriculum will be the reversal of this trend. Nursery education provides the foundations of children's school experience. These foundations must be built on and developed.

5
ASSESSMENT AT KEY STAGE 1: CORE SUBJECTS AND THE DEVELOPMENTAL CURRICULUM

Marian Whitehead

> Our nets define what we shall catch.
> (Elliot Eisner, 1985, p. 7)

The core of this chapter may be found in the epigraph which links, metaphorically, approaches to assessment with fishing nets. The aptness of the metaphor has been increased, rather ironically, by the slippery, protean character of the chapter topic which has proved almost un-nettable! The assessment of the core subjects at key stage 1 has been the subject of public controversy, pilot trials, despair, rethinks, ridicule, rumours and speculation for more than a year. However, at the time of writing – a phrase which has become tedious although invaluable – it seems that teacher judgements and greatly simplified SATs will be the main features of key stage 1 testing. This news has been greeted by general relief, if not elation, but serious professional questions about the nature and effects of assessing a core curriculum still remain unanswered, and even unasked.

The current emphasis is almost entirely on the search for 'simplicity' in testing tools and procedures and, by implication, on methods for checking up on what teachers have taught. But what will we really know about the children we teach when all the tasks are graded and all the other teacher assessments are collated? We shall probably know a lot about what teachers did. We shall know something about what Karin, Cassy or Katy did, to cope with the tasks and the testing. Will we know and understand, however, anything more about the children's own insights, reflections and strategies for learning? The following discussion aims to keep such awkward questions 'up front' by reviewing the nature of the National Core Curriculum, and by exploring the likely effects of national testing at age seven on the children tested, on the core subjects, and on the foundation subjects.

The starting point for this endeavour is a set of holiday snaps: a reminder of what children at the end of key stage 1 are like, as they demonstrate understanding and learning outside the school and the testing situation. It is, as Chapters 3 and 4 have already predicted, a picture of considerable complexity and sophistication and it provides a realistic basis for the ensuing discussion.

HOLIDAY SNAPS

Snap one: A hot summer morning on the beach and three girls, one six-year-old and two eight-year-olds, are making rather puzzling use of the family beach towels. They are totally preoccupied and seemingly working to the point of near exhaustion, piling sand on the towels and then dragging them, by gripping the four corners which are held together to create a basic 'sack', closer to the sea's edge. Sometimes the girls help one another with this strenuous task, but generally they all seem to have a fairly accurate idea of the maximum amount of sand they can drag. Indeed, as a stranger and an observer, I am so struck by this weight-dragging aspect of the activity that I have already presumed, teacher-like, that this is maths and technology in action. Clearly the girls are finding out just how much sand they can pull along and also how much strain the fabric of the towels can bear before disintegrating. The children are definitely interested in both these factors and they are particularly intrigued by the gaping and thinning effects of stress on the weave of the towelling. This latter phenomenon also interests and alarms a watching parent who reminds the girls that their 'experiments' might result in no beach towels for the remainder of the holiday! But it is at this point that the children's rejoinder demonstrates that I and their protesting parent have quite misunderstood the point of these strenuous efforts. The children's main purpose was to create a soft sandy path from their part of the beach to the water's edge. The broad expanse of beach closest to the sea was of gravel and the girls were laying a sandy causeway across this sharp surface so that entering and leaving the sea would be more comfortable.

Snap two: Another day, but the same beach and the same three girls, this time playing in the sea with an inflatable air-bed. The activity is apparently one of impressive physical skills and sheer delight in swimming, diving, floating and splashing. But the laughter and squeals of pleasure are in fact merely punctuating a sustained and complex fantasy narrative. Playing with the air-bed in the sea is the obvious activity but the three girls are creating, through talk and appropriate actions, a saga of 'rescue at sea'. Their clambering on and off the float and their headlong plunges into the waves are narrated as life-threatening but thrilling incidents: 'we're sinking', 'we're letting in water', 'bale it out', 'there's too many people on board', 'someone's fallen overboard', 'help, help', 'we need rescuing'. The language of danger and of rescue at sea is accurate, technical and highly reminiscent of adventure-book language. The game continues and renews itself for hours: each rescue is followed by yet more dangers as the over-burdened air-bed buckles, turns turtle and plunges out of control in the warm shallow water.

Snap three: Crossing the hotel gardens early one morning before breakfast I notice two small boys, probably six-year-olds, behaving very strangely. They are moving along the open staircases and walk-ways which link the individual apartments of the hotel and apparently being rather silly. One child is effectively blindfolded by the hands of his companion and is guided along, up and around the building complex by shouted instructions – and much giggling! Suddenly it comes to me that I have heard these cryptic instructions before: the boys are playing at computer 'turtles'. They take it in turns to be 'blind' and the guiding child shouts the computer instructional language of 'forward three', 'back one', 'left two' and the child-turtle takes the appropriate number of paces in the required direction. Like all young children, these two sometimes confuse 'left' and 'right' but this only adds to the fun and hilarity of the game, particularly when they react with excessively grovelling apologies to the door, wall or railing into which they have blundered.

These incidents were great fun to happen on, and writing about them has certainly made me long to be on holiday again. But what serious insights can a professional teacher gain from them? First, they were out-of-school, informal observations and yet they suggest a very powerful input from the early years of schooling. Apart from the obvious lessons with floor turtles and computers, there is evidence of the subtle influence on language and thinking of experiences with story books and narrative. This is shown in the air-bed adventures. The children's initiation into the technical and scientific processes of observing, testing and problem-solving, is revealed by their strategies for moving heavy loads and building a foot-friendly pathway to the sea.

Second, the children's considerable knowledge is unrecorded (apart from the fluke of a holidaying education tutor) and unassessed, and would not easily be described in terms of National Curriculum levels, but it is knowledge none the less.

Third, in these holiday incidents it is possible to identify elements of what we might call school subjects, for example, mathematics, science, technology, and language (English). But they are all interlinked, not only with one another but with drama, humour, social competence, imaginative thinking and physical skills. To comment only on the mathematics of the road-building episode, for example, would be to ignore and lose the quality of the language, the problem-solving and planning, the social negotiations, the science, the humour and the clear sense of purpose to which all of this endeavour was directed.

This brings me to a fourth insight for the teacher: all these activities were focused on solving the children's own problems and satisfying their own purposes and interests. These children were extending their knowledge, trying out ideas and exploring the possibilities of everyday life. This insight leads me to claim that they were playing. So far, in describing my holiday snaps, I have left this most obvious claim until late in the day. Yet all the insights I have suggested pick up on the complexity, creativity, independence and freedom from external pressures of the children's holiday activities. Of course they were playing! Freed from the need to conform to arbitrary and imposed standards for satisfactory performance in moving sand, laying paths, floating on and capsizing air-beds, or locating one's hotel room, these children extended their bodies, their minds and their understanding of a range of facts and phenomena, beyond anything that could be demanded in a test.

Finally, another obvious insight, the children were on holiday in family groups and relaxed and caring adults were always around. Sometimes these carers were just watching on the periphery of the play, sometimes they offered practical help, advice and warnings. The moments shared between the adults and the children were rich in allusions to previous family history, experiences and knowledge. This reinforced my own sense of the children as operating effectively and adventurously from a safe base in the shared world of family relationships, community and culture.

Showing holiday snaps is usually a guaranteed way of boring friends and ruining a social occasion. However, I have risked all this in order to demonstrate, very tentatively, what might be described as a holistic approach to observing young children. This 'method' – already too rigid a term – seizes the moment; takes all and any activities as grist to the mill of deepening existing knowledge about children; lays down few parameters or time limits; and seeks to avoid precipitous assumptions and tidy categories. It attempts to capture just a fleeting sense of the real, 'felt on the pulse', nature of childhood – and adulthood. The insights I noted earlier are an indication of the rich data which the most informal of these kinds of observations can yield. It is from this starting point that I wish to move on to a theoretical and practical consideration of the formal requirements for assessing the National Curriculum core subjects at key stage 1. The children I met on holiday were coming up to, or just past, this key stage and their demonstrated knowledge, problem-solving and play provide the 'touching base' aspect of the following discussion.

DÉJÀ VU AND THE NATIONAL CURRICULUM

My dictionary claims that the experience of perceiving a new situation as if it had occurred before, *déjà vu*, is sometimes associated with exhaustion and certain mental disorders. It would be easy enough to attribute the feeling, widespread among educationists and teachers, that we have met the National Curriculum before, to sheer exhaustion and mental confusion. But, in the interests of historical accuracy, it must be said that the rationale, the priorities and much of the content of the National Curriculum have been imposed on generations of teachers and children in the past. We are experiencing not so much the perceptual confusions of *déjà vu*, as the faint memories of 'old, unhappy, far-off things/And battles long ago' (Wordsworth).

Recent commentators (Aldrich, 1988; Kelly, 1990) have unerringly identified the National Curriculum as a direct descendant of that mid-Victorian curriculum which was designed to gentle the masses, to produce clerks and factory hands, while still keeping expenditure on elementary education down to a minimum through a system of 'payment by results' (Revised Code, 1862). This is the background against which Kelly (1990) charts the historical and conceptual developments which have culminated in a great shift of focus enshrined in the 1988 Act. This allegedly 'new' and 'reforming' legislation is in reality a volte-face: suddenly the direction of education has undergone a complete about-turn, a turn taking it away from the 1944 Education Act's conception of education as a social service and a right for all, and back to those older notions of educating the masses for 'industrial training and social obedience' (Kelly, 1990, p. 34). All this has been accompanied by speedy legislation which does not leave any time or opportunity for thorough debate about the purposes of education. Indeed, such prickly questions as who is education for, what is it for, what is it like, how do we know when, or if, it has happened, have been sidestepped. You will not find them in a search through the ring-binders. What you will find is an official view and a set of priorities which constitute the rationale for the

National Curriculum, but there is no serious analysis of the nature of education. It is the aim of this section to highlight the official National Curriculum 'priorities' from a specifically early childhood standpoint and indicate some causes for real concern.

The first general point has already been made, that the National Curriculum 'is at least 83 years old' (Aldrich, 1988, p. 22). Like its Victorian ancestor it is dominated by two major concerns: economic accountability to those in power outside the profession, and the summative testing of pupils at regular intervals. The introduction of market values into education is now well under way and the economic competition which is openly encouraged does raise central issues about 'what' and 'who' education is for. Very young children may not appear to be caught up in the struggles for free filofaxes, lavishly carpeted classrooms and good jobs, but they are powerless and at risk if the acquisition of such 'goodies' is taken to be the main purpose of education.

At the very beginnings of pre-school and statutory schooling it is essential to focus on first things first: 'authentic education is committed to the pursuit of understanding and to the recognition of values' (Abbs, 1990). This approach is not a naive or hypocritical condemnation of the marketplace and material success, but a reminder that the self-worth and happiness of those who eventually go to the market must be established first.

It is not only the 'Hard Times' principles of schooling, economic accountability and market values which lead professional educators to view the National Curriculum as inappropriate for the 1990s (NUT, 1990). The inescapable facts are that the 'new' curriculum is dominated by traditional assessment and subject content. All teachers must now be quite clear that standardized assessment, that is testing, is the central purpose of the National Curriculum. This needs to be clearly understood if strategies for supporting, and even educating, young children are to be evolved. 'Criterion-referenced assessment (especially if very detailed and requiring the full attainment of each separate criterion) is bound to produce an assessment-led curriculum . . . This is what they are designed to do. They are intended to narrow down what it is possible to do in the classroom to the achievement of specific objectives – and not others' (Kimberley, 1990, p. 22). Kimberley goes on to spell out the message even more starkly in its implications for the individual teacher and pupil: this strong form of assessment 'leaves no room for manoeuvre – you either achieve a target or level, or you don't' (ibid.).

While getting to grips with the nature of this curriculum we need to realize that its central concern with assessment is linked with specific views about what is to be assessed. The National Curriculum is a content curriculum based on a fairly narrow conception of traditional school 'subjects'. I use the term 'traditional' advisedly because the same subjects dominated the syllabus in secondary schools in 1904 (Aldrich, 1988). It is reasonable to suppose that an old secondary curriculum 'tapestry' 'of vertical subjects and horizontal themes is an unsatisfactory model for a school curriculum that should provide flexibility in the face of change' (NUT, 1990, p. 12, 3.8). It is likely to be an even less satisfactory model for the early years of education which are concerned with very young children's first-hand experiences and their development of understanding in broad areas such as the human, social, literary, linguistic, mathematical, scientific, aesthetic, moral, physical, technological, and so forth.

Schools are already beginning to move away from these modes for organizing human experiences and are taking on a subject timetable mentality of 'things to do to cover the targets'. This trivialized approach to planning for teaching is becoming increasingly common. An education supplement in a 'quality' national newspaper has devoted a whole page (the pages may be photocopied for classroom use) to carrots! Carrots for science, technology and design: these 'did you know that you can make interesting designs by printing with a piece of carrot' gimmicks are reminiscent of the dreary object lessons promoted in the last century. The arbitrary class lesson is back and is one of the rash ways in which desperate teachers will attempt to 'cover' attainment targets. I have not yet seen every child drawing and labelling the parts of a wilting buttercup, but I have seen class lessons on the naming and drawing of geometrical shapes and the reintroduction of 'phonic' word lists to learn for homework.

The assessment requirements of the National Curriculum focus on the isolation of discrete 'markable' tasks which are then aggregated as batteries of attainments. Chapter 1 has analysed the shortcomings of this approach in a broad educational context but, in the early years specifically, such an approach undermines the holistic model of the child developing into a thinking person which my 'holiday snaps' attempted to capture. An obsession with testing not only disrupts the teacher–child partnership in learning, as well as spoiling many other planned educational activities, it fails to assess the most important of cognitive activities. What are of proper professional interest to the educator are the links that the young learner is creating between different phenomena, experiences, feelings and events. Learning and thinking are always about creating knowledge by a process which makes sense of the new in terms of previous experience; it is a process which transforms all previous understandings and knowledge. In other words, thinking and understanding are bridge-building activities which link domains, they are not a kind of master-mind approach to collecting approved lists of facts.

It has already been noted that you either achieve a target or level, or you do not (Kimberley, 1990) and, similarly, you either know a list of facts, a geometric label, a phonic 'sound', or you do not. A curriculum dominated by criterion-referenced, summative assessments certainly gives children plenty of opportunities to fail. Many teachers have already pointed out that the one thing the new assessment procedures and targets are very good for is defining what children cannot do. These particular 'nets' are catching a lot of stunted and frightened small fry which should at least be thrown back and allowed to grow a little bigger. After all, we are talking of key stage 1 children who are only eighty-four months old! This is a depressing thought, as Waterland (1990, p. 5) has noted in respect of the reading requirements: 'The only child whose label will be even half-way accurate is going to leave school one day in early July with a written report telling him, his family and anyone else who finds out, that Lenny is a failed reader'. The new emphasis on getting things right will militate against acknowledging complexity and variability in learning and it will undermine a proper intellectual respect for the young learner's inexperience and areas of 'not knowing'.

The need for teachers of key stage 1 pupils to have completed charts of attainments for every child in all of the core and foundation subjects, and to have tested them in the core subjects with nationally standardized tasks, will inevitably change priorities and activities in the early years. I have already referred to a probable trivialization of the curriculum, but there may well be a worrying change in the relationships and status of learners and teachers. The pressure for assessment in the early years is likely to marginalize interactive teaching and learning styles based on the Vygotsky model. This emphasizes children's potential and highlights the sophisticated levels they can reach in thinking when supported by an adult partner (Vygotsky, 1978, 1986). If key stage 1 children, and this silly label is also likely to stick, are judged on a 'can do/cannot do' basis, their teachers are also likely to be judged simplistically and consequently de-skilled. The teachers have already been designated as 'deliverers' of the curriculum and few other transport or postal workers require a four-year further education course in order to deliver packages. The excessive emphasis on assessment could also make the teacher's task both simpler, because less dependent on complex professional judgements, and less worthy of respect. Perhaps anyone who is 'good with children' at an intuitive level will do for teaching, once the reflective, analytical and truly 'professional' elements of the job have been made redundant. 'In no time at all it will be apparent to the world at large, and rightly so, that anyone can supervise worried and nervous little children doing their tests. And anyone can mark and grade with the aid of answer books, league tables and lists of established national standards' (Whitehead, 1988, p. 71). We have indeed 'been here before' but a closer look at the terrain might help us to ameliorate our stay and even plan a new world.

THE FIRST DIVISION CURRICULUM

At the time of writing the nature and extent of the statutory SATs at key stage 1 have just been announced. Interestingly, the announcement in a national publication is illustrated by a cartoon of a stereotypical boffin Secretary of State for Education, complete with spanner, tinkering with a nineteenth-century cast-iron machine running on cog-wheels and pulleys. Perhaps our fun and jokes tell more of the truth than we dare to admit? Every picture tells a story and this one suggests that the curriculum is a machine designed in the last century to produce a specific item. Furthermore, this end-product can be changed or modified, by a little judicious tinkering with the right nuts and bolts. If we stay with the metaphor, we not only have our main production line in education which is driven by the core curriculum machine, we are also permitted to struggle on with an inefficient side-line in decorative knick-knacks, or 'foundation subjects', which can be bolted on to the end-product if required. My 'nuts and bolts' analogy may be seen as a little exaggerated and unkind, but thoughtful analysts and commentators have not hesitated to point to the two-tier nature of the National Curriculum and its related assessment procedures.

It is impossible to deny Robin Alexander's claim (1990, p. 16) that 'the persistence, and indeed celebration by the National Curriculum, of the gross discrepancies between what I call Curriculum I and Curriculum II, or the basics and the rest' surfaces in any analysis. It is present in the terminology of 'core subjects' and other foundation subjects; it is underscored by official decisions to test only the core subjects at key stage 1; it is further emphasized by the reduction of SATs to a pattern of basic reading, writing, arithmetic and some science. The discrepancy between the basics and the rest is also reflected in the lack of agreement and guidance on analysing and assessing 'the rest', apart from technology which originally seemed likely to be designated a core subject. Sadly, this constant harping on a core of basic subjects emphasizes the utilitarian flavour of a National Curriculum which is not even 'national' but public sector and, apparently, aimed at producing a competent industrial work-force. This sense of fairly arbitrary promotions and relegations of subjects, based on little more than respect for traditional school subjects and a belief in the virtues of fierce competition and classified results, has led me to think about the situation in terms of League Division Football tables. Such a metaphor is valuable precisely because it is shockingly inappropriate as a way of discussing the early education and life chances of very young children. Metaphors are creative tools for thinking because they link disparate worlds of experience and throw up new connections, relationships and insights. Metaphors also provide symbols which can stand for the intangible, the complex and the inarticulate. Thinking about the core curriculum in the early years of schooling in terms of Division One, or the First Division, helps to clarify what effects there may be on the subjects included in this division, as well as on those subjects relegated to the Second Division.

The Education Reform Act (1988) and a number of DES advisory documents require that pupils receive a broad and balanced curriculum. Apart from the strong inference that pupils are passive receivers of the curriculum package, theoretical analysis and classroom observations reveal that the two-division curriculum is difficult to broaden or balance. The apparently enlightened list of subjects masks the imbalance produced by statutory requirements for public testing and assessment in the core subjects. Any hope that the National Curriculum could have been a broader, richer and balanced experience for most children is undermined by an analysis of the spread of subjects across Divisions One and Two. This is particularly clear if we switch our attention from discrete subject titles and focus on broad curricular areas; humanities, arts and sciences, for example. On this analysis the core of basics in Division One consists of two scientific areas, mathematics and science, and a 'humanity' with arts connections, English (and Welsh in Welsh-speaking schools). In Division Two the relegated teams represent three humanities, religious education, geography and history, plus Welsh in English-speaking Welsh schools; two arts, music and art; and another one, or even two, scientific areas. These are technology, now named without 'design', its visual arts and humanities link, and perhaps physical education, although it certainly has aesthetic aspects and is significant in personal development. Thus the problems of balance and breadth are starkly exposed: most of the humanities and arts components in the National Curriculum are relegated to the Second Division. The plight of these inevitably devalued subjects will be discussed in a later section, along with the implications for young children's learning experiences in school. But even the core itself, with its emphasis on scientific ways of thinking, is further distorted by its Division One status and all that flows from that.

First, because English, mathematics and science are lumped together as 'basics', it will be the minimal, over-simplified and 'basic' features of their content and processes which will become high-status. It is the basic bits of the basics which are already becoming highly regarded, tested nationally and discussed publicly. One of the great lost battles of the Education Reform Act is the imposition of the label 'English' on the broader, richer conceptions of language in human development and thinking formulated by many professional linguists and educators. The special case of Welsh in Wales throws up many confused and insensitive attitudes to language and culture held by those who assembled the National Curriculum. Welsh is a core subject in schools which are Welsh-speaking, but it is to be made a compulsory foundation subject in the 5–16 curriculum in English-speaking schools in Wales. This is an attempt to force culturally distinct groups of pupils and teachers (and families) to become unwilling bilinguals – in the interests of national identity! Yet the National Curriculum is generally inadequate or silent on the linguistic status and rights of the many genuinely bilingual children in our schools in England and Wales.

This unacceptable official confusion about the nature of language, identity and self-image results in a total lack of consistency. The Welsh language juggernaut rolls through English-speaking schools in Wales, but the English language steamroller rolls over those children in England and Wales who are speakers of Hindi, Turkish, Urdu, Italian, Arabic, Sylheti, Greek, etc., etc. Furthermore, by actually naming 'English' as a core language component for all schools we lose a crucial perspective on the central role of any human language in cognition and personal and cultural development. This loss has been borne out by recent reports on the SATs to be used in 1991. Despite the powerful contribution made by the Cox Report (DES, 1988c) towards a proper emphasis on talking and listening, literature and narrative, and children's highly creative approaches to becoming literate, the standard tasks will be a conventional reading test, writing, spelling and handwriting.

In mathematics basic computation and operations on numbers appear to predominate, with just a cross-section of experiences with shape, space, collecting data and measuring to be tested. It is easy to see how in practice this is likely to downgrade, or exclude, any focus on play with mathematical ideas, the beauty of pattern and number, and the nurturing of mathematical thinking. Similarly, the testing of science is already emphasizing content and method at the expense of passion and curiosity. Perhaps there is a real danger that only those children who do *not* experience core curriculum science will have any chance of becoming scientific thinkers:

> We had the *Encyclopaedia Britannica* at home. When I was a small boy he used to sit me on his lap and read to me from the *Britannica*. We would be reading, say, about dinosaurs. It would be talking about the *Tyrannosaurus rex*, and it would say something like, 'This dinosaur is twenty-five feet high and its head is six feet across'.
> My father would stop reading and say, 'Now, let's see what that means. That would mean that if he stood in our front yard, he would be tall enough to put his head through our window up here.' (We were on the second floor.) 'But his head would be too wide to fit in the window.' Everything he read to me he would translate as best he could into some reality.
> (Feynman, 1988, pp. 12–13)

Feynman goes on to mention, in parenthesis, that he learned very early the difference between knowing the name of something and knowing something (op. cit., p. 14). These telling anecdotes carry important messages for professional teachers who are committed to a developmental curriculum. Effective learning, that is, learning which extends beyond the confines of schooling, emerges from meaningful interactions with caring and involved adults. Such learning is supported and extended by talking, reading and the creation of metaphors and analogies drawn from daily realities. For all of us, at any age, the process is one of making sense of new content knowledge in terms of what is known and part of our lives already. But at no time is this more important than in the early years, when the temptation to overwhelm young children with what they do not know and to underestimate what they do know, is very great. The central problem inherent in the National Curriculum and national testing, and the central difficulty for this volume, is located in this temptation – a temptation made almost irresistible by the imposition of subject content and summative testing on the early years curriculum.

At this time certain quick and easy but very unwise solutions to the problem are being put forward and practised in schools with children coming up to key stages 1 and 2. 'Knowing the name' of things is making a comeback, as has already been mentioned. Two- and three-dimensional shapes, digraphs and initial and terminal letter-strings, spellings out of context and rules for computation are frequently 'taught' as whole class lessons. This claim is based on personal observations but it is not intended as an attack on teachers, who find it increasingly difficult to circumvent the 'input' emphasis of a 'transmission of content' type of curriculum.

Another very popular and 'simple' solution gaining ground is that of baseline testing. This proposal arises from almost undeniable logic and good intentions, and confronts two significant early years issues. First, on entering statutory schooling young children are not starting from the same place or stage in development. (Note the interesting metaphor: is education a race, and to the victor the spoils?) Children have individual developmental differences and special needs; they have different experiences of early nurture, socialization and pre-school learning; they have experienced profoundly different social, cultural, religious and ethnic assumptions and life-styles. Some children will have had variable periods of time in nursery education, some will have attended play-groups, some will have had none of these pre-school experiences. The second issue relates to the purpose of national summative testing which is, presumably, to demonstrate what children have learnt in the key stages, or how far they have progressed. Given the different starting points reception children reveal on entering school, how can tests at age seven indicate the real progress they have made? The answer appears obvious: test them first on entry at four plus or five years of age. But, test them on what? The core curriculum subjects they have not actually been taught? Should we resort to unreliable IQ tests and non-verbal reasoning games, or dig out the old 'Reading Readiness' protocols? All these so-called tests are notoriously culture-specific and have biases which condemn many children to fail, sometimes simply because they have not encountered a tea-table laid with cups and saucers, or bought a single biscuit for 5p with a 20p coin. (Try that transaction in the local supermarket!) Baseline testing falls into the trap of all non-diagnostic summative tests: it is good at producing failures and locating apparent falls from arbitrarily established 'standards'. The special horror of baseline testing is the probable identification of infant failures who are only sixty or fifty-four months old.

The section on 'Ways Forward' will return to this worrying issue of establishing baselines, but within a more positive context, and Chapter 6 will develop the possibilities of helpful practices in teacher-led assessment of children.

THE NET AND THE CATCH

The SATs designed to test some of the attainments of seven-year-olds in English (or Welsh), mathematics and science are a net in which we are now able to catch what children can do, or, more exactly, what seven-year-olds in public sector schools should be able to do. The change from 'can' to 'should' is deliberate, for there can be little doubt that a system, which is designed to facilitate the publishing of test results widely, will rapidly blur the distinction between stating what 'is' and stating what 'ought' to be the case. SATs test children's performances on certain attainment targets in the core subjects; SATs imply a particular view of children as learners; SATs are nationally applied in the public sector and the results are to be published. They are, in fact, 'exams' for seven-year-olds: 'they are there to see that the curriculum is taught' (Gipps, 1988, p. 69). They are also sure to create a popular taxonomy of what every seven-year-old should know; they will define the average key stage 1 level 2 child.

So, now that the net is in place, we know that the 'average' seven-year-old should be able to: describe current work in mathematics, record findings and check results; read, write and order numbers to 100; solve whole number problems involving addition and subtraction, including money; distinguish between odd and even numbers; show understanding and experience of handling data and predicting the outcomes of events; work with 2 and 3D shapes; know the most commonly used units of measurement . . . In the exploration of science, learn to plan, hypothesize and predict; design and carry out investigations; interpret results and findings; draw inferences; communicate and discuss work; know something of the processes of life; know something about human influences on the earth; be able to group materials according to their characteristics . . . In English, use pictures, context and phonic cues for reading; listen and respond to stories, poems and other material read aloud and express opinions about them; write stories with an opening, characters and events; produce recognizable spelling of common words; produce capital and lower-case letters in handwriting and use them appropriately . . .

A first glance at these targets may cause most of us to declare 'I've been teaching the attainment targets all my career without knowing it', with the same degree of amazement felt by the character in Molière's *Le Bourgeois Gentilhomme* who discovered that he had been speaking 'prose' all his life and not known it. However, 'our nets define what we shall catch' (Eisner, 1985) and unexceptionable as these specimens are, for many are quite acceptable and useful, they are still a collection of isolated and limited objectives. If 'catching them' is all there is to the exercise it is doomed to be trivial, telling teachers nothing they do not know already and wasting the children's time. Professional teachers need to know far more about the contexts in which their pupils can or cannot 'do' certain things. Such contexts will be social, physical and cognitive, and constitute a total conceptual framework for talking about and assessing knowledge in the areas of language, mathematics and science. There is a considerable body of research which shows that young children's demonstrated knowledge is radically affected by the social and physical constraints of their immediate surroundings (Heath, 1983; Tizard and Hughes, 1984; Wells, 1985; Barrett, 1989). A long tradition of cognitive and linguistic research suggests that children's thinking is at its most powerful when engaged with real problems and discrepancies which are broadly linguistic, mathematical or scientific, and frequently all three at once (see Vygotsky, 1978; Bruner and Haste, 1987; Wood, 1988; Pellegrini, 1988; Athey, 1990).

These, perhaps, are 'the ones which get away' when we use the National Curriculum net: social and physical factors, the need to engage with genuine problems and questions, and the broad conceptual frameworks which lie behind school core subjects. In using the term 'conceptual frameworks' I am thinking of the kinds of theories of the world and of human experience and understanding which underpin mathematics, language, literature and science. These 'subjects' are in fact ways of knowing and organizing the world, and these ways of 'coming to know' (Salmon, 1980) are acquired gradually. Therefore, the early years practitioner must monitor and record the child's current mathematical, scientific and linguistic view of the world and chart the child's learning strategies and achievements so far. This highlights once again the significance of teacher assessments and judgements in the early years, and will be the subject of the following chapter. However, the issue of teacher assessments of the total curriculum is particularly problematic when a very limited range of children's isolated attainments is to be tested nationally and probably published. What exactly is the status of the far more wide ranging and subtle teacher assessments, and what opportunities will there be for teachers to explain and demonstrate these to families and communities? It is quite clear that professional teachers do need to go beyond the requirements for national testing if they are to understand children's linguistic, mathematical and scientific ways of thinking.

If the National Curriculum net is designed only for a limited catch, some other ways of netting the rich potential of children's thinking must be devised. Ways in which we might create these other nets will be indicated at the end of this chapter, but as a preliminary we need some notion of the rich catch which might be getting away from the existing key stage 1 net. Three major losses at the key stage 1 phase of testing could occur: first, evidence of the distinctive modes of thinking which develop when the conceptual frameworks of the culture continually re-structure children's perceptions and thoughts; second, evidence of children's potential and the existence of a zone of proximal development in thinking and learning

(Vygotsky, 1978); third, awareness of complexity as the distinctive feature of the teaching and learning situation.

In order to consider the first possible loss – evidence of conceptually distinctive modes of thinking developing in early childhood – we could start with mathematics. Children's mathematical thinking arises from an early sensitivity to space in relationship to their own bodies, to sound and movement, patterned repetitions, order and sequence. These kinds of awareness fuel a drive to sort out and organize objects, persons, experiences and phenomena. This early thinking is supported and extended by cultural and social interactions which encourage sorting, grouping, matching, naming, counting, ordering and quantifying people and things. The more specifically mathematical skills of numeracy and measuring build on the active 'doing' which typifies the mathematical thinking of the child in the nursery, or the children on holiday portrayed at the start of this chapter. At this point in mathematical development it is crucial to resource early years and pre-school classrooms with the appropriate materials which stimulate and extend mathematical understanding.

> This development can best be encouraged by the provision of a quality of open-endedness. Only one size of plate in the home corner, only one selection of vegetables, only one possible landscape for the miniature world of the farm, or only one assortment of Lego bricks or large construction bricks – all these will restrict the answers to any possible questions and, as a consequence, the depth and richness of the child's mathematical thinking and the potential scope for his or her development.
>
> (Metz, 1988, p. 189)

The child's earliest number experiences, and most of our daily adult counting and number 'operations', are rooted in the solving of practical problems. How many candles on your birthday cake? How many teaching weeks until the end of term? How many leaves did we collect in the playground? Was it really 'hundreds'? How many 20p coins for the tube fare? This is all mathematics and it is all real problem solving which we can engage in from the earliest years without feeling deskilled and unable to 'do mathematics'. Perhaps the problems arise because, as Metz indicates, 'An emphasis in education on applying rules in a step-by-step manner ignores not only the need to make general sense of a situation first, but also the importance of reflecting on any solution obtained after the rules have been applied' (ibid, p. 187).

Making general sense first and later reflecting on solutions points up the links between scientific, mathematical and linguistic thinking. All are ways of making sense of the world of people and things, they are modes of understanding, not tricks to be taught and then tested. This warning applies particularly to early approaches to science because there is a danger that the methods and assumptions typical of secondary school science will overwhelm the primary curriculum. There is ample experiential and anecdotal evidence of teachers 'doing experiments' in front of watching infants and then asking them to draw and write about these scientific experiences. Hands-on science must involve more than the teacher's hands. In fact, lively investigative problem-solving science has been going on in early years classrooms for generations. For example, Susan Isaacs (1930), Teddy O'Neill (1977), major national projects (Science 5–13, Richards *et al.*, 1972) and countless other teachers, have helped young children to collect, observe, hypothesize, test, consider variables and formulate their scientific understandings. These successful and honestly scientific approaches have capitalized on young children's desire to touch, taste, watch, explore, talk about, dismantle, draw, collect and organize their immediate surroundings. Such approaches have been most typically resourced by the 'everyday bits and pieces surrounding children, for specialized equipment often comes between children and understanding and can isolate the science from a child's real world' (Richards, 1988, pp. 229–30).

The real world for all of us is to a great extent created and organized by language, and young children's language reflects their developing mathematical and scientific understandings. Language itself develops a dual inner and outer function which structures rational thinking, and colours thoughts and feelings with the social experiences, beliefs and assumptions embodied in human languages (Vygotsky, 1986). Language is a tool for learning and teaching, for individual thinking, for social communication and for carrying the distinctive conceptual frameworks of mathematics and science. But language, literacy and literary forms are also distinctive ways of perceiving the world and discussing the chances of life: the 'human condition' so often mentioned by literary critics. Children are part of this language process from the moment of birth when adults greet the newborn and introduce them to a world of human expectations, values and motives: 'Who's a grouchy baby, then? Hasn't she got her granny's stubborn chin?'

The stories are a lifetime's business, and a complex web of talking and listening, reading and writing extends the potential we all have for creating the meanings which transform happenings, instincts and accidents into accounts of lives and relationships. Small children do not just look at pictures in books, nor do they 'talk in simple terms' (AT2) about characters and content. They recognize objects, people and animals and link them with events, feelings and attitudes which have preoccupied them: 'My cat's like that one, but my cat died.' 'She's sad, isn't she?' 'My mum don't let us go up the market 'cos it's dangerous.' Every teacher receives these evaluations daily but perhaps they are not always respected as powerful modes for thinking about the chances of life; for recognizing the symbolic representation of ideas, feelings and events in books or told tales; and for sharing and modifying views of the world. This listening, talking, gossiping, rhyming and dramatizing about life occurs in any language, not just English, and these ways of thinking are not likely to be amenable to national testing at key stage 1. In a way this is splendid news, a guarantee that they will not be ticked off on checklists and grids. But, in another way, it is rather worrying because they may be demoted and marginalized along with all the other Second Division subjects.

If the breadth and depth of the distinctive mathematical, linguistic and scientific modes of thinking are at risk of missing the National Curriculum net, and thereby being lost or diminished, the notion of children's potential is even more endangered. Professional teachers have always been aware of the need to tap children's potential and good practitioners have always held high expectations for their pupils. However, it is only in recent years that the work of Vygotsky on 'the zone of proximal development' (1978) has begun to reach practising teachers. Jerome Bruner (1986) and James Britton (1987) have explored the significance for pedagogy of this exciting yet realistic notion. In essence it reaffirms that we need to pitch our teaching and provision just beyond, or at least on the edges of, a child's current developments and achievements. However, we also need to support the child in crossing this zone from the point of 'can do with help' to the stage of 'can do alone'. Such a notion lies behind the provision in nursery and infant classes of writing areas and the materials for creating lists, labels, letters and messages. Furthermore, the 'exploiting' of willing helpers who can write already and act as enthusiastic scribes, interpreters and readers is one practical extension of the theory. Similarly, adults share books with children who are not yet independent readers and use the metaphor of 'apprentices and experts' to describe their approach.

The dynamic forward thrust of this kind of teaching for potential is also enriched by the provision for, and observation of, children's play. In play it is as if the child were a head taller, functioning at maximum potential and demonstrating where his or her thinking and investigations are moving forward (Vygotsky, 1978). The dilemma for the early years educator who works within the statutory National Curriculum stages is that SATs and statements of attainment may create a ceiling on teaching and learning at various stages and levels. The dangers of teaching and testing just to the required levels and targets is insidious and must be countered by a very conscious sense that in school 'the sky is the limit'.

There are many examples in the DES literature relating to key stage 1 of references which use the term 'simple': respond to simple instructions, talk in simple terms, read simple signs, spell simple monosyllabic words, use a simple dictionary, identify simple differences and properties. Yet it is widely acknowledged that children's thinking is far from simple (Bruner, 1983; Wood, 1988; Pellegrini, 1988). It may be qualitatively different from adult thinking, sometimes based on limited experiences in the world, but it is a complex amalgam of observations, explorations, emotions, language and cultural assumptions. Early problem-solving by young children, as demonstrated in first language acquisition, playing, drawing, writing, reading and spelling, is characterized by highly creative abstracting, hypothesizing, constructing and revising. Similarly, early years classrooms are complex human environments in which the dynamics of relationships and interactions are negotiated. Early years learning has this in common with all human learning: it is profoundly affected, for good or ill, by powerful subjective issues such as self-esteem, respect, commonsense understandings, non-verbal communication and unarticulated attitudes and prejudices. Very young children can become just as disaffected from schooling as older children and adolescents (Barrett, 1989). Yet another aspect of complexity which young children engage with, although the testing of children at seven may not indicate this, is the conceptual frameworks of mathematics, science and language and literacy. These have already been discussed but should be added to a tally of what are not simple but, on the contrary, complex features of young children's thinking in and out of school.

These possible losses from the net created by the National Curriculum assessment of core subjects are significant. Without them one can hardly begin to plan for Monday morning. Furthermore, the lack of such rich data makes us easy victims for those who regularly cry 'falling standards' whenever learning is related to everyday human understandings and made enjoyable. One can counter such responses only from a position of knowledge about human learning and thinking, knowledge about young children's development, and knowledge about the nature of knowledge itself. Unfortunately, many of the decontextualized and cryptic shorthand phrases for sensible practices which occur in the National Curriculum ring-binders do hold the profession up to ridicule. There is something very silly about spelling it out in such naive detail, for example: 'pick up books and look at the pictures' (English AT2).

The very fact of focusing highly publicized SATs on only a small section of school learning diminishes the importance of the teacher assessments across the broad and balanced curriculum. It also over-simplifies and trivializes the core subjects so that they are perceived as sums, reading, writing, and a few science tricks. Saddest of all, the National Curriculum league table approach has created a Second Division of relegated subjects.

IN THE SECOND DIVISION

Some major problems surround what Alexander (1988) called Curriculum II: the arts, humanities, and personal, moral and social education. The existence of these problems has been a constant theme running through the previous discussion. First, these areas of knowledge are outside the high status core and therefore downgraded. Second, little clarification exists about what they involve in terms of early learning. There is also a third dilemma posed by the very fact of describing the early years curriculum as lists of discrete subjects. Are we proposing that the generalist primary teacher is an expert in history, geography, art, music, religion and technology, as well as in English, mathematics and science? And are some primary teachers in certain areas of the United Kingdom automatically bilingual Welsh/English speakers? Or are we accepting the beginnings of an introduction of subject-specialist teachers across the whole primary range? The latter route would be totally destructive of an early years tradition which seeks to nurture young children's development, in a holistic fashion, through the range of social, cultural, cognitive and affective dimensions. More importantly, it would be seriously damaging to the quality of life of very young children in schools.

Professional early years carers and educators must still base their expertise in child development and an understanding of the relationships between curriculum and developmental modes of thinking and creating knowledge, as many contributors to this volume assert. We cannot sensibly claim to be specialist historians, artists, or whatever, and nor should we wish to, for we are skilled practitioners of a different sort. This may question the appropriateness of timetabled subject slots in the early years curriculum, but it does not undermine the immense significance of the arts, the humanities and the moral and social dimensions of human ways of knowing. Indeed, highly schematized sets of 'facts' about history or geography, for example, can be understood only if they are first rooted in young children's curiosity and discoveries about other times, other places, other people and other traditions. The sense of time and of place for the young child springs from knowing and sharing family history, anecdotes and gossip, as well as local places, local photographs and personal archives and artefacts. Through these encounters real knowledge of subjects is created, not delivered. What other way is there?

Well, there is the way of relegating many subjects to a Second Division in the curriculum league and 'doing' them piecemeal. In claiming, as this chapter does, that the foundation subjects are inevitably downgraded by this approach one is forced to consider what could be lost or damaged. Evidence that major areas of knowledge have been devalued, or are in danger of being lost, is provided indirectly by the National Curriculum documentation on cross-curricular themes and personal and social education. It is as if, having imposed a worryingly disparate and bitty model of knowledge and curriculum, the DES is now supplying 'holistic glue' in a hasty attempt to urge us to put the kit together! A Second Division curriculum is unlikely to be effective, in the early or the later years, because it is not simply the case that subjects like art and physical education will be forced to the edges of the timetable, or themes like moral and social education be omitted. The current pattern is marginalizing not just a set of subjects and themes, but major modes of knowledge and understanding. This claim addresses my second problem, set out at the beginning of this section, the lack of clarification about what the relegated subjects entail in terms of early learning.

From the perspective of early learning and the developmental curriculum it is possible to clarify at least four immensely significant features of the Second Division curriculum. First, several of the subjects constitute major forms of symbolic representation; second, they include the basic mode of early learning through exploratory movement and action. Third, these subjects involve culturally created forms of knowledge and identity; and, fourth, personal and moral development is entailed in all of them. This is not to suggest that the core subjects do not also have some elements of these significant features, but the features are richly exemplified in many of the 'at risk' components of Curriculum II. Without this richness the core itself is weak.

The significant role of symbolic representation in thinking and the organizing of experience into forms of knowledge is central to any concept of education. Infants move rapidly on from being totally dependent on present and actual objects and situations, in order to express their desires and observations. Facial expressions, body movements, gestures, the making of graphic marks and drawings, play and pretence, precede and then run alongside language as symbolic ways of 'standing for' ideas, feelings and activities. The young child who places a cereal bowl on her head as a 'hat', or makes vigorous swirling marks in a patch of spilt drink is representing for personal contemplation notions, perhaps of hats as objects seen on heads, or, in the latter case, strongly felt experiences of movement and speed. For the infant, living must seem to be a positive maelstrom of fleeting images, sensations and stimuli, but the wet marks linger and the bowl 'stays put' long enough for these notions and sensations to be held and preserved. This urge to preserve, contemplate and celebrate is common to play and the arts, to drama, religion and history, and certainly to much of science and technology. Designing a solution to a problem or a felt need is possible because of symbolic representation. For example, generations have gazed at the birds and cultures have created tales of people who fly – disastrously or successfully. Very young children still run and flap their arms or improvise billowing 'superman' capes; older children experiment with paper darts; Leonardo da Vinci draws a possible flying machine; and the Concorde flies the Atlantic on a regular schedule.

Experiences of body movement, physical exploration and energy were mentioned in the previous comments on symbolic representation. Theories of representation and symbolizing are linked to the claim that early learning is a matter of internalizing actions as images, mental representations and thoughts. Manipulating and managing objects and one's own body precedes and makes possible the manipulation of symbols, or ideas, about people and the environment. These theoretical claims remain powerful for the later stages of learning: we continue to organize hands-on experiences with materials, information technology, art techniques and a wide range of practical skills. In the early years we demonstrate the significance that movement and action has for cognitive as well as healthy physical development, by planning for outdoor play in a challenging environment, and for physical education with specialized apparatus. We support and extend children's learning with opportunities to play, to build, to pretend, to experiment, to make, to dance, to dramatize and to have hands-on experience of science, practical mathematics and problem solving. We do not do this because the Second Division curriculum is good for keeping children 'busy', but because this curriculum is the source of human thinking through action.

Many of the relegated subjects in Curriculum II are deeply rooted in cultural ways of seeing and describing the world. Like the languages of the core curriculum, history, geography, art, music and religion (and Welsh) define unique human characteristics and cultural groups. For all of us, our sense of self and of self-worth is intimately bound up with a group past, a common territory, and a pattern of significant seasons, celebrations and rituals which shape our lives. Young children are initiated into these national and ethnic forms of knowledge by growing up in family groups and knowable communities. Experiences in school should aim to broaden, enrich and confirm children's sense of identity and worth, by opening up even greater vistas of human diversity through history, geography, religious belief, aesthetic expression and cultural tradition. This sets a very high standard for these domains of knowledge and it will not be attained if we are reduced to doing some rather limited singing, some projects on Romans and Victorians, and 'the story of a bottle of milk' – if and when the time table allows. Children in the early years accept that the world of people, events and things is weird and wonderful. Schooling should be bold and innovative enough to extend the wonder and explain the weird. The curricular ways of doing this exist, but they are now concentrated in the Second Division curriculum.

Educators of any seriousness at all are concerned for the personal and moral development of those they educate. This note of earnestness can be mocked and such related notions as educating 'the whole child' may be criticized at this point as empty jargon. However, personal and moral development are matters rated highly by parents and communities who still look to schools to provide some lead in establishing 'good' behaviour, respect for others and 'right' attitudes. These expectations may appear to be vague but they are voiced by very diverse cultural, ethnic and social groups. In recent discussions with key stage 1 class teachers in inner city areas it was made clear to me that parents still worry more about children's behaviour and personal development than about the effects of testing at age seven. Problems with attitudes and behaviour are the commonest reasons the parents give for wishing to see these teachers about the children. Given the significance of these concerns, we can only note that many opportunities to address personal and moral issues arise from those subjects which are now grouped in the Second Division of the curriculum. With the notable exception of literature, the humanities and creative, social, personal and moral issues are 'relegated' in the new national structure.

This brief look at the wider significance of the Second Division subjects indicates that they are areas of knowledge and ways of thinking which are centrally important for human development, in the early years and later. It also suggests that promotion from Division Two should be effected immediately. A positive note at last! We do have to teach on Monday morning and we must offer the youngest members of society hope and a worthwhile school experience – worthwhile here and now at ages three, four, five, six or seven, as well as having potential for a future we cannot predict or guarantee in any detail. There must also be professionally positive ways forward for teachers of key stage 1.

WAYS FORWARD

The start of this chapter laid down a 'real world' base from which the arguments could be launched: some informal holiday observations of children at play. Now the time has come to 'touch base' again and attempt to create some positive suggestions for ways forward in assessing the core subjects, ways which are firmly rooted in a holistic approach to observing and teaching young children, despite all the dangers of fragmentation inherent in a subject-based approach.

Many commentators have decried the lack of any educational philosophy, rationale or theoretical dimension to the National Curriculum and have urged the construction of this missing foundation as the basic task for every teacher. To this end, work on disseminating the approach exemplified by the London-based Primary Language Record has led to the development of a Primary Learning Record (Barrs *et al.*, 1990). This initiative aims to assist teachers by establishing clear guidelines for cross-curricular assessment and record-keeping which are grounded in the processes of learning. The emphasis for the teacher is on making observations, gathering evidence of progress, reflecting on the evidence, and using it for forward planning (ibid., p. 38). The emphasis for the learner is on a learning continuum, an interweaving of five dimensions of learning: confidence and independence, experience, strategies, knowledge and understanding, reflectiveness. This work is well known among early years practitioners and will be analysed in the following chapter but it also bears a striking resemblance to the evolving views of subject specialists who are now developing approaches for the primary years. Although the work is aimed at the junior years, there is much to applaud and develop in, for example, the STAR (Schilling *et al.*, 1990) approach to primary science. The emphasis is on an active, investigative style which singles out for assessment the processes of observing, interpreting, hypothesizing, planning, measuring, recording, raising questions and critically reflecting (op. cit., p. 26). These processes are also identified in the National Curriculum, Exploration of Science, Attainment Target 1, and raise the issue of our perceptions of teaching science in the early years. Providing that we do put our main classroom emphasis on 'doing' science and finding it all around us, we should avoid the pitfalls of teaching isolated facts about magnetism, buoyancy, or genetics, which have no context for very young learners – as yet.

Teachers of children who are starting key stage 1 need to judge where the children are at in their learning development and they also need to create classroom contexts for extended learning in the core areas. Their priorities must be, first, the collecting of detailed observations of children, individually and in group situations, and the early tapping of valuable parental and family knowledge about individual children; second, the creation, maintenance, and development of a richly resourced classroom environment which is full of appropriately focused language, mathematics and science. The earlier comments on the Second Division should have made it clear that the classroom and the school should also be a place of potential and actual art, drama, history, geography, technology, play, physical education, dance, music and ritual. It is only within such varied learning contexts that one can hope to find out what children know and understand presently; along what lines their thinking and investigations are beginning to take them; what they need to know next; and which attainment targets have been hit (and at what level). Furthermore, baselines need not be tests for the early diagnosis of 'inadequacies' brought from homes and cultures, indeed they *must not* be such damning exercises. Concern with baselines should be focused on the children's own current knowledge and interests and should respect these as the rich matrix from which development is evolving. The required model is not a deficit identity tag but something akin to the early language learning pattern.

One recent example of work on a book-centred approach to baseline assessment in language (Crossland, 1990) does appear to be positive and nurturing and demonstrates the special quality of young children's language learning. At its best it is confident and risk-taking and used with great skill 'to explain, organize and elaborate ideas, to open up and go beyond what was given' (op. cit., p. 51). When this powerful tool of language is used to explore and organize the mathematical, scientific, or other curricular areas, the gains may be similar. Other researchers describe it as a process of opening up children's language in response to the possibilities of the broad early years curriculum. These ideals of expansion and growth in language and learning depend for their realization on flexible and sensitive professional teaching in schools: 'the openness of language leads to both creativity and error. That the process which leads to creativity is also the process which leads to error is something we must accept' (Harste, Woodward, Burke, 1984, p. 129). The notion that creative or open-ended approaches to learning have a potential for error and involve risk-taking applies to all aspects of learning right across the curriculum. Getting it wrong stimulates new insights in literacy, in scientific hypothesizing and in mathematical problem solving. But this can only be an insightful process if error is not threatening but seen by the learner and the teacher as a source of new discoveries. In the context of a National Curriculum dominated by testing and a 'stage' theory of summative hurdles at seven, eleven, fourteen and sixteen, professional teachers will have to defend the values of error and 'not knowing' very stoutly indeed.

A tradition of stout defence and vitriolic counterblasts is not strong among teachers: we tend to go in for weary resignation but we have developed an amazing ability to work in 'the spaces' (Jones, 1989). Although this beavering away in the spaces between bureaucratic legislation and paper-work may be criticized, it is a classic professional skill. We practise the art of good teaching despite the demands that we fill in forms and checklists and apply in triplicate for essential equipment and resources. In the age of the National Curriculum this skill in teaching despite the 'other demands' is likely to become the essential attribute of the good practitioner. This idea is gradually gaining acceptance as many teachers evolve a philosophy of hanging on to appropriate, well-resourced, wide-ranging and open-ended teaching, carefully geared to individual differences – then translating the outcomes into National Curriculum terminology. The approach is clearly demonstrated in the work of the Early Years Curriculum Group (1989) which uses the learning webs favoured by many early years teachers and nursery nurses for curriculum planning, and then superimposes on these indicators of the relevant National Curriculum attainment targets.

Just as working 'in the spaces' left by legislation is no longer a rather weak response but a positive professional strategy, so working across the curriculum is becoming respectable at all stages and advocated by HMI and NCC. Early years practitioners are the archetypal cross-curriculum experts and in responding to the stress of so many timetabled 'subject' demands they are reassessing the appropriateness and flexibility of this early years tradition. Cross-curricular themes and projects do not have to be invented or copied from NCC guidelines, they are suggested daily by the children we teach, if we make time to watch, listen and respond imaginatively to their concerns. The most ordinary event will open up extraordinary possibilities across the curriculum. A playground in November covered in drifts of fallen leaves can lead to classroom and school work on change, decay, seasons, time, leaf skeletons, animal skeletons, counting to high numbers, covering and comparing areas, regular and irregular shapes, symmetry, comparing and ordering sizes, stories, poetry, music-making, vocabulary extension, evergreen and deciduous plants, wood technology and construction, planting tree seeds, studying birds and squirrels, life-cycles and ecology . . . Most of the curriculum is in there somewhere but, very importantly, this starting point is rooted in wonder and delight, in sensory explorations and in children's love of collecting things.

So, what might an appropriate net for the core of subjects in key stage 1 look like? The short answer is that it would look like a developmental assessment model in which assessment is primarily ipsative, or child-referenced. A cyclical model is best suited to ensuring that the outcomes of assessment do feed back into a continual updating of the professional teacher's knowledge about individual children and groups. The cycle should involve the following closely linked stages:

- observation: in order to capture the child's-eye view of problems, tasks and strategies;
- interaction: records of child–adult learning partnerships and child–child interactions;
- feedback: between learning partners, this involves professional subjective judgements;
- recording: a major stage which preserves information for review, analysis, the detection of patterns of development or difficulty. But this must include children's choices and self-assessments and the contributions of parental or family views and evaluations;
- progression: the 'what next' issue and the business of professional judgements again! These judgements lead to modifications and innovations in teaching, planning and provision. Then back to 'observation' of teaching and learning initiatives and modifications.

It is the purpose of the next chapter to develop detailed considerations of teacher assessment but this suggested net for the core subjects is made from a three-ply twine. There is the thread of professional judgements, the thread of teacher and learner critical reflectiveness, and the thread of good early years practice. Targets and tasks play a minor part in the creation of the appropriate net.

SUMMARY AND CONCLUSIONS

A discussion centred on creating an appropriate net for an un-nettable catch was bound to be somewhat negative. However, the dilemmas raised by assessing the core subjects in the National Curriculum must be faced and resolved if education, rather than mere schooling, is to be offered to children at any key stage.

The chapter began with glimpses of an informal, real-world context which might help to illuminate any discussion of young children's skills and achievements. This was followed by a brief historical overview which was intended to clarify our understanding of the origins and assumptions which lie behind the current National Curriculum model. The remaining sections raised the central issues of the chapter and these issues certainly bear repeating in summary form.

First, the main success of testing at key stage 1 is likely to be in the identification of what children cannot do: that is, the simplistic labelling of lack of competence. Second, this testing approach will probably neglect the nurturing of individual potential and marginalize those supportive learning partnerships which take all of us beyond the limits of our isolated abilities. Furthermore, it is apparent that the required system of assessment will not be able to cope with complexity, idiosyncrasy and the uniqueness of individual learning biographies.

The decision to test only the core subjects at key stage 1 confirms a curriculum league table approach: the First Division subjects are to be tested by SATs. Correspondingly, down in the Second Division, 'the rest' of the foundation subjects will not be subject to statutory testing. This procedure will yield a new classification of school knowledge which will eventually harm, distort and isolate even these core subjects.

There is now a real danger that the pressure of this subject and content-oriented curriculum in the infant school will bear down on, and restrict, nursery and pre-school curricula and provision. The warning signs have appeared already: there are calls for baseline testing at four-plus and five years of age, and there is a huge expansion in privately run pre-schools with an avowed emphasis on 'establishing the basics' and getting infants ready for the National Curriculum.

This discussion has not been wholly negative; it has reasserted some strong professional claims: first, that early years teachers must preserve a richly varied curriculum; second, that they must assess and record appropriately, as befits a developmental approach; and third, that they must identify and report on the required targets and levels of attainment *after* learning, teaching and education have had a chance to become established.

In conclusion, it is important to assert that the claims and criticisms of this chapter do not come from the wilder shores of eccentric educational theory. There is a substantial groundswell of informed opinion, based on years of classroom research, coming from those countries which have a long tradition of centralized school curricula and extensive testing, that theirs is not the path to take, or continue along. The North American experience is highly relevant here. After years of tightly controlled class-room programmes, frequently administered standardized testing procedures, basal readers and schemes of all kinds, the teachers and the researchers are saying that assessment must be broadened. It must be opened up to encompass and honour the whole of a child's qualities and modes of knowing (Marcus, Feldman and Gardner, 1988). American teachers are being urged to ask themselves what the tests they use so rigorously actually tell them about their students' abilities to pose interesting questions, solve out-of-classroom problems, think in serious and sustained ways, and be reflective and self-evaluating (Wolf, 1988). New Zealand educators are now in the midst of national curriculum innovations and many distinguished early childhood practitioners are voicing fears that the drift towards skills and content-based tests is inappropriate and counter-productive (Carr and Claxton, 1989). These international perspectives suggest that we must return to the task of publicly communicating our child and learner-centred approaches. The need for an educationally informed public debate and a developmental curriculum 'voice', or rhetoric, is as urgent here as on the other side of the world, or the other side of the Atlantic. This chapter is a contribution to the rhetoric and a warning of the dangers inherent in certain curriculum developments at home and abroad:

> Simple theories have led to simple-minded instruction. The result is a profession and a nation at risk; restrictively labeled children, educators, and education.
>
> (Harste, Woodward and Burke, 1984, p. xix)

6
ASSESSMENT AT KEY STAGE 1: TEACHER ASSESSMENT THROUGH RECORD-KEEPING

Sue Pidgeon

Teachers in early childhood education have a fundamental responsibility for the all-round development of the children they teach. Therefore each child's development is at the heart of any assessments.

Assessment and record-keeping have always been a part of a primary teacher's work. They are powerful and important because it is the assessments that teachers make about pupils' progress that allow them to plan and make provision for individual children's development. This is the crux of formative assessment.

Although teachers' assessments of their pupils have always been part of teaching it is only in the relatively recent past that there has been interest in developing educationally valid and useful forms of recording children's development, and an acknowledgement of the importance of this. However, this evolution has been abruptly hijacked by making teacher assessment a statutory part of the National Curriculum. As part of mandatory assessment at the end of a key stage teachers must record children's levels of achievement in each of the relevant attainment targets, and these combined with the SAT scores give the overall level the child has achieved. Teachers are also expected to have in place systems of record-keeping that enable this teacher assessment related to the National Curriculum to be carried out throughout the years of schooling to provide continuity.

But children's development is not some simple, vertical progression. The complexity of young children's learning and development has been outlined earlier in this book. In the previous chapter, Marian Whitehead makes clear that at key stage 1 assessments of children need to be holistic and developmental and to include all aspects of children's learning.

This chapter looks more closely at teacher assessment and record-keeping at key stage 1. First, it will consider the development of teacher assessment, the principles underlying it and what it could look like in practice. Then it will go on to look at the present situation in relation to the National Curriculum and focus on the problems inherent in this, and possible solutions.

WHAT IS TEACHER ASSESSMENT?

Assessment is an integral part of the teaching and learning process. Teachers are constantly making on-the-spot judgements about pupils' learning and progress, and then using this assessment to inform their teaching. Teachers in the early years have always been concerned with the whole child's development and so their judgements will encompass children's cognitive development but will also include their social and affective development as well. This circular process of planning for the pupils, the pupils working, the teacher making assessments and feeding these back into the planning must take place for teaching and learning to be effective. This would be the case at any age or level. It can be represented by a simple diagram (Figure 6.1).

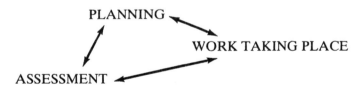

Not every assessment needs to be recorded. In fact, many informal assessments teachers make do not need to be recorded, and certainly have not been in the past. But if these judgements are to be more than fleetingly useful, then some kind of record will need to be made of significant assessments. If this record is going to be useful, then it must be in a form that is both manageable and informative.

Such records will build up into a continuous ongoing profile of the child's progress over time which can be shared with the child, parents, teachers and others involved in the child's progress. The TGAT Report (DES, 1988a, para. 3) says 'promoting children's learning is a principal aim of schools. Assessment lies at the heart of this process'. But it must really be considering teacher assessment because only that can provide the broad picture of the child. Certainly this is implicitly acknowledged in official publications. The DES document 'From Policy to Practice' (DES, 1989b, para. 6.5) says: 'Teachers' own assessments are an essential part of the system. They will be able to cover aspects of performance not readily testable by conventional means and more generally will ensure a place in the assessments for rounded, qualitative judgements. Most teachers will not be starting from scratch in carrying out assessment and recording of pupils' achievements. This is already part of good practice in primary and secondary schools'. The SEAC booklet *A Guide to Teacher Assessment, Pack C* (SEAC, 1990b, p. 6) says 'Teacher assessment is a rich source of information about the child'. So it seems that it is agreed that teacher assessment is an important and integral part of the education process. It is not something 'extra' that is added at the end of the day or year or key stage. Nor should it lead the curriculum. Instead, assessment should be built into the ways that schools, pupils and teachers work (SEAC, 1990a). In this way teacher assessment is developed from many existing forms of good practice, and becomes part of an integrated framework for planning and working in schools and classrooms.

Teacher assessment through record-keeping is a crucial part of the teaching and learning process. But what is actually involved?

There are two distinct activities: first, gathering the information or evidence about what the pupils are doing; and second, making a judgement about it. Significant assessments will then probably be recorded. Teacher assessment is teachers making professional judgements about the children they teach, and recording them. These are not objective measurements, and there is much evidence to show that teachers' judgements are a more effective form of assessment than standardized tests. Unfortunately, much of this work has been undermined by the emphasis in the National Curriculum on testing as a way of judging children's progress.

The strength of teacher assessment is that it allows teachers to build up a picture of the whole child, but the kinds of assessment teachers make will reflect their view of teaching and learning. So, for example, when assessing young children's writing, if the prevalent view is that the way children form their letters is what is important, then that is what teachers will assess. The kinds of assessment made and records kept are linked to thinking about learning and teaching, and these will change over time. Teachers' assessments can be as broad or as narrow as anyone wants, but in order to be of value they need to be considered fair against defined procedures and criteria. Recent important work has been looking at ways of agreeing and defining procedures and criteria because, if teachers' assessments and records are going to be useful in a formative way, they need to be within a clear and coherent framework. There has been a move away from both very broad generalizations (for example, 'Sarah is a bright and lively child'), and narrow assessments (for example, a reading age of 6.3 years) to looking to develop frameworks to record and assess the underlying processes of learning. This change in approach to assessment and record-keeping in schools coincides with schools and LEAs becoming more aware of the need to have coherent curriculum statements that allow for children's development throughout the primary years and the importance of monitoring progress within this. There has been much discussion among staffs to establish curriculum policy statements and the criteria for assessing and recording children's progress. Also, the increased awareness of the importance of parental involvement in children's progress in school has extended to assessment and record-keeping. The records need not only to be shared with the parents (and the criteria for making the assessments made known to them), but parents, too, can contribute to the records of their child's progress, as can the children themselves.

Methods of record-keeping have evolved alongside teacher assessment. Records need to be able to indicate what children have achieved, and so be sufficiently informative to allow for future planning. They need to be collected regularly. Individual records of assessments may soon be outdated as children will be developing and changing, but they will build cumulatively into a profile of the child and record the child's achievement over time. Because these will be records of broad and holistic assessments, then various ways of recording the information may be used, and will need to involve teachers, parents and children.

The two main practical considerations are that the assessment procedures and the keeping of records must be easy to carry out as part of normal teaching and that they must not be too time consuming. The records need to cover both the content and process of children's learning.

The last twenty years have seen real developments in thinking about teacher assessment. Assessment has become less tied to selection (as in the days of the 11+) and more about recording pupils' achievement, so the teacher's role in assessment has become more important. (This is reflected in the GCSE examinations, in Records of Achievement in secondary schools and in the Primary Language Record (CLPE, 1988.))

PRINCIPLES UNDERLYING TEACHER ASSESSMENT

Although work on teacher assessment has been somewhat fragmented, it is possible to establish certain principles that should guide valid practice.

First, teacher assessment and record-keeping are part of normal work in the classroom. They are not tests either of the child or the teacher but should take place in a normal classroom setting. They should reflect good primary practice, so, for example, they allow room for collaborative learning, discussion, etc. Teacher assessments need to be ongoing and cumulative and need to assess the child in a variety of contexts. This fits in with good practice in early childhood education, so, for example, any assessment of children talking would not only be made on a straight question-and-answer session with the teacher but would look at the child talking and listening in a range of contexts and social situations, say, in imaginary play, in a problem-solving task, in small and large groups, etc. This allows for a broader picture of a child's competencies to build up.

Second, teacher assessment needs to be holistic and to look at the learning process as a whole rather than the end product. This is certainly very much in line with a developmental approach to learning that means that teachers are looking not only at what children have achieved but at the learning processes involved. This means that teachers are going to be making more descriptive observations of what children can do rather than what they cannot do. They will therefore need a system of recording that allows for this. Records have moved away from simple tick-sheets to a format that will be formative and reflect the process rather than the product of learning. The way that teachers record children's reading development is a good example of the change in recording systems. A child's reading record used to consist solely of the date, the book and the page (e.g. 10 April, *Billy Blue-hat and the Duck Pond*, Book 2a, p. 6) and included nothing about how the child was reading. As teachers have become better informed about the reading process through work by Smith (1985), Meek (1982) and Holdaway (1979), then obviously they need a record to reflect this. Linda Yard in Wade (1990) describes how a group of teachers

> . . . began to notice that, although no two children developed in exactly the same way, some developmental stages were common to many children. We wondered if we could present these observations in a way that would be helpful to us and to other teachers. The document we produced, 'A developmental record of emergent reading', is the result of many meetings and much discussion and redrafting over an initial period of two terms and during a pilot year involving 75 teachers using the record alongside the weekly records of 2,400 children. We now feel confident that it is a useful resource for

individual teachers and for a whole school policy of assessing reading development.

(Wade, 1990, p. 162)

A record like this (Figure 6.2) is an attempt to cover, in a non-linear way, the many aspects involved in the reading process.

Third, all those involved in the children's learning should be involved in the assessments. This can mean all those working with the child at school, as well as the parents and the child. One of the major changes in assessment in recent years has been the realization of the importance of involving pupils in their own assessments. Work (mainly in secondary schools) that has been done on this shows that pupils become more involved in and reflective about their work and this benefits their learning. Many secondary schools have developed Records of Achievement that include pupils' own assessments. This is acknowledged by SEAC (1991) in their recommendation of Records of Achievement as a form of ongoing record for primary schools.

Also, the awareness of the important role parental involvement plays in children's progress in school has extended into assessment and record-keeping. The records can be shared with the parents (and the criteria for making assessments need to be made known to them), and they can also contribute to the records themselves.

Fourth, the children need to understand clearly what is required of them when assessments are being made. This is particularly important at key stage 1 when children are being initially introduced to the 'school view' of the world.

When children start statutory schooling at five they enter a strange new world that is governed by assembly and playtime, and particular ways of behaving in the classroom. Even those children who have had experience in a nursery class will notice the change. So, children in school at key stage 1 are learning from the context of the school as well as through the curriculum. Sometimes there is a mismatch between what the child perceives as the task, and what the teacher does. Work by Tizard and Hughes (1984), Wells (1985) and Heath (1983) makes it clear that the way in which learning is perceived at home is very different from the way in which it is perceived at school, and that teachers may sometimes make inaccurate assessments of children's progress. An example from a student's work on a child's reading will serve to illustrate this. The student was working with Jason, a Year 1 child, and had assessed him as having very little knowledge about reading and print because, despite becoming familiar with several books, he showed little interest. However, by chance she brought in a tape recorder, and was most surprised when Jason was quickly able to point out

This record sheet is intended to be used simply as a guide. We emphasize that we believe emergent reading follows no linear progression and that the sequence of development is unique for each child.

	ATTITUDE TO READING		
Observes shared reading	Sharing 1 to 1 willing to hold book	Sharing 1 to 1 comments on picture/story details	Relates own experience listening 1 to 1
Sharing 1 to 1 willing to tell story first to adult	Concentrates and enjoys a story in a group	Concentrates and enjoys a story read to class	Chooses to share a book with an adult
Enjoys illustrations as an integral part of the story	Mulls over picture details	Chooses to browse through books alone	Handles books with care

Keeps returning to special books he/she can really read	Looks for books by favourite authors	Discusses story in detaiI	Looks for favourite sets of books	Returns to favourite books	Enjoys sharing a story aloud with friends

Willing to tackle an unseen text	Eager to read part of a new story to others	Enjoys reading known texts aloud with expression	Browses with friends –shared enjoyment	Enjoys reading silently

Figure 6.2   A developmental record of emergent reading

Source: Wade (1990) Reading for Real, pp. 104–5 used with permission of Open University Press.

PRINT AWARENESS
Aware of some public print

INCREASING PRINT AWARENESS

Aware of initial letter of own name	Recognizes own name	Notices print around classroom

SHARING 1 to 1

...turns pages accurately with help to find beginning	...turns pages accurately	...predicts during first reading	...joins in repeated sections	...echoes adult reading

RE-TELLING A STORY

Turns pages randomly commenting on pictures	Consistently looks at left hand page first	...Relates it to own experiences	...with accurate page turning commenting on some pictures	...with accurate page turning, inventing own story

INCREASING PRINT AWARENESS

Looks for words beginning with initial letter of own name	Recognizes names of some of friends	Identifies some print in the classroom	Some sight vocabulary of high interest words

RE-TELLING A STORY

...uses picture clues	...in own words sequence correct	...in own words and some book language	...accurately from memory	...accurately pointing towards but not focusing on print	Is able to focus on print

...finger scanning direction correct but not focusing on print	...finger scanning matches first and last word, one line phrase	...finger scanning left → right left ⟋ right correct	...memorises simple text and matches words 1 to 1	...known text matches words making contextually correct guesses	Place: holds with finger

INCREASING PRINT AWARENESS

Emphasizes changes of type in the print	Begins to notice words that are the same	Begins to notice punctuation	Aware of some initial sounds	Knows names of some letters	Known text uses initial letter clues

Realizes when comes across unknown words	Self-corrects using initial letter clues	Self-corrects by re-reading part of phrase or sentence	Some sight vocabulary	Notices patterns within words	Aware of some phonic clusters

BEGINNING OF INDEPENDENCE

Takes over from adult on initial reading of text	Able to tackle unknown text

If the document is used as a development record we suggest that a diagonal line is made across the specific rectangle when the behaviour is first noticed and a further line added in the opposite direction when the behaviour is a definite part of the child's development. We suggest the use of pens of three different colours, for example; red for reception, green for middle and blue for the top year.

the brand name and which button said 'start'. Further investigation made it clear that Jason had a lot of knowledge about reading environmentally based print. What he did not have was much familiarity with books, and the student's first assessment had been skewed because she had only viewed 'reading' from the school's point of view. Walden and Walkerdine (1982) have also looked at this, particularly in relation to children's mathematical work, and suggest that what may appear to the teacher to be the child's lack of understanding is sometimes because the children are confusing the context of the task with the content. The following example from their work illustrates this:

> In the following dialogue the P2 teacher talks to a girl, Kathy, who needs help with a question on her work-card.
> T: Right, where have you written your answer? You've got 'How many conkers weigh the same as five shells?' There's no answer written. Have you done it?
> K: (shakes her head)
> T: Now, you're not sure how to do it? Right. Will you go and put five shells on one side of the scales and then get your conkers ready and I'll come and see you.
> K: How many conkers shall I need?
> T: Well it says – the question is, 'How many conkers weigh the same as five shells?' So you've got to find out how many until the – it's what? If they weigh the same what do the scales look like? Are they up, down, or straight?
> K: Straight.
> T: Straight. You've got to see how many conkers you've got to put into the other side until they're straight, and then when it's straight you come and tell me; alright?
> After this exchange, Kathy went off to try and complete the task. She did not, however, count out a number of shells or conkers, but repeatedly raised and lowered the fulcrum of the scales in an attempt to make it go straight . . . Kathy continued with her quest to find the answer and became very distressed at her repeated failures in the attempt.
> (Walden and Walkerdine, 1982)

Kathy's problem had been in her misinterpretation of the teacher's explanation of the task and in putting all her efforts, not into finding the correct number of conkers, but into straightening the balance.

The child had been confusing the context of the task with the task itself. The teacher, in her attempt to clarify the concept of 'weighing the same as' had focused on the scales being straight. The child had taken the straightness to be the content of the task. Once in school, children are introduced to concepts with which they are already familiar from pre-school experiences (e.g. weighing, reading, measuring) but in a more formalized way, and this can lead to misunderstandings and confusions on the child's part. This again means that it is important that teacher assessments at key stage 1 allow for analysis of the learning processes and are not reliant on superficial impressions.

A point arising from this is the importance of speaking and listening at key stage 1. Many of the teacher's assessments rely on children understanding instructions or on interpreting what children are saying. Again, it is absolutely right that speaking and listening are the language modes that are predominantly used to assess children, as they are the ones young children are most familiar with and competent in. However, teachers need to be aware that teacher and child may not always share the same understandings. This is particularly important when working with bilingual children, when an early stage of knowledge of English must not be confused with an early stage of cognitive development. This will be developed in the next chapter.

This leads on to the fifth principle, that *teacher assessment needs to take account of equal opportunities* in terms of gender, race, class and special needs. It is notoriously difficult to eradicate bias from assessment and many forms of standardized assessment have been proved to be biased. This is an area that often is not considered seriously and yet has significant effects on pupils' progress. Even now, *The Times Educational Supplement* (5.4.91) reports, 'Ministers have vetoed a research project aimed at cutting racial and sexual bias in school examinations because they were not convinced that such discrimination actually existed . . . But the schools Examination and Assessment Council has now resubmitted its equal opportunities project in the light of new evidence reported by the *TES* in February that the GCSE has widened the gap between boys and girls and different racial groups'.

Teachers need to be aware of areas of possible bias when making assessments. This means ensuring that the materials used and the curriculum on offer reflect the multicultural society and are relevant to all pupils.

Also, the teacher's interaction with the child affects the teacher assessment. Both the teacher's perceptions of the pupil and the style of teaching will have a bearing on this. Certainly teachers' perceptions of children will also be influenced by their preconceptions in terms of intelligence or gender, race or class. Bias can be counteracted by including procedures for moderation of teachers' assessments. The preferred method at key stage 1 would be by involving teachers as moderators, possibly supplemented by external moderators. Moderation helps to strengthen perceived validity of any teacher assessment.

So let us reassess the principles underlying teacher assessment. Teacher

Primary Language Record

School	School Year

Name	DoB	Summer born child
	☐ Boy ☐ Girl	

Languages understood	Languages read
Languages spoken	Languages written

Details of any aspects of hearing, vision or coordination affecting the child's language/literacy. Give the source and date of this information.	Names of staff involved with child's language and literacy development.

Part A To be completed during the Autumn Term

A1 Record of discussion between child's parent(s) and class teacher *(Handbook pages 12-13)*

Signed Parent(s) _____   Teacher _____

Date _____

A2 Record of language/literacy conference with child *(Handbook pages 14-15)*

Date _____

© CLPE/ILEA 1988, 1989

Figure 6.3   Excerpts from the Primary Language Record

Reprinted from the *Primary Language Record* by kind permission of the Centre for Language in Primary Education, Webber Row, London, SE1 8QW

3 Reading Samples (reading in English and/or other community languages)
to include reading aloud and reading silently

Dates			
Title or book/text (fiction or information)			
Known/unknown text			
Sampling procedure used: informal assessment/running record/miscue analysis			
Overall impression of the child's reading: • confidence and degree of independence • involvement in the book/text • the way in which the child read the text aloud			
Strategies the child used when reading aloud: • drawing on previous experience to make sense of the book/text • playing at reading • using book language • reading the pictures • focusing on print (directionality, 1:1 correspondence, recognition of certain words) • using semantic/syntactic/grapho-phonic cues • predicting • self-correcting • using several strategies or over-dependent on one			
Child's response to the book/text: • personal response • critical response (understanding, evaluating, appreciating wider meanings)			
What this sample shows about the child's development as a reader. **Experiences/support needed to further development.**			

• Early indicators that the child is moving into reading

Figure 6.4   Excerpt from the Primary Language Record

assessment can provide a broad picture of a child's progress. Assessment and record-keeping are part of normal work in the classroom. Teachers' assessments and records should be related to the curriculum studied, and the criteria for making the assessment need to be clear not only to the teachers but also to the children and the parents. The assessments and records should build into a broad profile of the child that will be shared with the child, the parents and the child's teachers. The assessments should be non-discriminatory and teachers need to be aware of issues of equality, such as race, class and gender. These are the principles. In the next section we need to go on to look at what teacher assessment and record-keeping are like in practice.

A MODEL OF TEACHER ASSESSMENT THROUGH RECORD-KEEPING AT KEY STAGE 1

Despite the work on teacher assessment and record-keeping there are few published systems that reflect the principles outlined in this chapter. One example that deserves closer scrutiny is the Primary Language Record (1988) later expanded to the Primary Learning Record (1990).

In the mid-1980s the Inner London Education Authority, as part of its commitment to improving primary schools (exemplified in the Thomas Report 1985), set up a steering group based at the Centre for Language in Primary Education to consider and develop an improved system for recording children's development in language and literacy that would reflect the existing good practice in schools. The good practice reflected significant developments in research about children's language and literacy development (for example, some teachers were using Miscue Analysis [Goodman, 1973] to give them a better picture of the whole reading process) and teachers needed systems of assessment that allowed them to record the teaching processes involved. After extensive discussion, drafting, piloting and redrafting, the Primary Language Record (1988) was published. It comprised a cumulative record (Figure 6.3) that charted development of children's reading, writing and talking over the year. It involved the teachers, the parents and the children and took account of bilingual children's development. It also included sampling and observation sheets (Figure 6.4) so that teachers could assess not only the product but the process of learning. These informal assessments would feed into the main record. The criteria for making the assessments were explicit on the record and sampling and observation sheets, and were elaborated in *The Primary Language Record Handbook for Teachers* (CLPE/ILEA, 1988).

The record has been enthusiastically taken on by teachers, who have found that their knowledge and understanding of their pupils' progress have been considerably enhanced. Meek, commenting on this, says:

> As a result, teachers discover how to observe their own interactions with pupils, the particular texts used in class, and to reflect on the nature of children's progress in reading and writing from the efforts of all who are involved. The Primary Language Record will change what comes to be regarded as evidence of what literacy is, not least because it comes from where the evidence *is* in the reading and writing lives of children, their parents and their teachers.
>
> Evidence of this kind has been available before now only in specialized research. Now it offers a means of both assessment and forward planning related to the actualities of learning. The words of children count.
>
> (Meek, 1990, pp. 145–6)

The record was used in ILEA primary schools from 1988 onwards. It was introduced to schools through a programme of in-service training that supported teachers' use of it. The abolition of ILEA in 1990 prevented the Primary Language Record from becoming the official record of that authority but its success has been phenomenal and its use has spread well beyond London, both throughout the British Isles and across the world.

The success of the Primary Language Record led the staff of the Centre for Language in Primary Education to extend the record to cover other curriculum areas in the same way and produce the Primary Learning Record (1990). This then provides a means for teachers to record children's cross-curricular learning within one record. The Primary Learning Record also takes on the National Curriculum requirements for teacher assessment and attempts to avoid the proliferation of different recording systems for different subject areas.

As previous chapters have made clear, young children's learning is not linear or simple. Most important about the Primary Language Record and the Primary Learning Record is that they are concerned with assessing and recording the breadth of children's learning experiences. They identify five dimensions of learning that are interconnected and underpin children's progress and development, and that the record takes account of. As Barrs *et al.* (1990, p. 35) say, 'All five dimensions form part of a continuum of learning: they go on being important and developing throughout a person's life as a learner'. These five dimensions are confidence and independence, experience, learning strategies, knowledge and understanding, and reflectiveness. By basing the records on a holistic, developmental view of learning, teachers are able to make educationally valid assessments.

The Primary Language and Learning Records have been described as an example of teacher assessment that exemplifies good practice at key stage 1. If teacher assessment through record-keeping is part of the National Curriculum we need to go on now to look at that in more detail to see how it fits with good principles and practices.

TEACHER ASSESSMENT AND RECORD-KEEPING AND THE NATIONAL CURRICULUM

The picture of teacher assessment given so far in this chapter is that significant developments have taken place in this area and that it is possible to develop models of record-keeping that take on the holistic nature of children's learning. This situation seems to be acknowledged by official publications quoted at the beginning of the chapter. But the reality of teacher assessment at key stage 1 is very far from this. The introduction of teacher assessment and record-keeping as part of the National Curriculum has followed none of the good practices described in the development and introduction of the Primary Language Record. There has been no guidance in terms of record-keeping, no consultation. The structure of the National Curriculum, being subject-based and tied to attainment levels, is in opposition to holistic assessment. Many of the suggestions that the TGAT Report (DES, 1988a) made for supporting teacher assessment have been lost, and the balance between teacher assessment and tests is constantly moving towards the latter.

In 1991, the first year of assessment at the end of key stage 1, the demands of teacher assessment seem to be causing confusion and hostility in teachers, many of whom have been actively involved in the positive developments in assessment prior to the National Curriculum. The experience of watching teachers in Year 2 classes in the spring term 1991 who had to complete assessments related to the attainment targets seemed to bear out all the concerns voiced throughout this book and particularly those focused on by Marian Whitehead in the last chapter. Good early years practice was quickly replaced by an assessment-led curriculum. In many classes children were ricocheting from one unrelated activity to another to ensure all attainment targets were covered; there was no time for children to learn in any meaningful way, things were just being 'taught' in ways far removed from good practice (for example, 'tens and units' off the blackboard!). Teachers' perceptions about assessment and their confidence in their own professional judgements seemed suddenly skewed. Some schools were suggesting that every piece of children's work should be kept and marked with an attainment target and level. (They were seriously suggesting that new stock cupboards would need to be built to accommodate all the evidence.) Teachers were limiting their teaching to the attainment targets in the three core curriculum areas, which meant children were having very limited learning experiences. The idea, too, that the programmes of study guided what was to be taught was quickly replaced by teaching the 'attainment targets' – certainly proof that what is to be assessed dominates what is to be taught.

It is worth looking in a little more detail at the contradictions that teacher assessment within the National Curriculum imposes on teachers. These concerns about the effect the National Curriculum will have on young children's learning experiences run through this book. The complex and conflicting interrelationship between the curriculum and assessment have been explored in Chapter 1. A National Curriculum is in place but there is no coherent theoretical framework for teaching and learning behind it.

The imposition of a ten-level subject-based curriculum is in direct opposition to all that has been established in this book about the developmental, cross-curricular, holistic nature of children's learning. As Barrs (1990, p. 43) says:

> Children approach their learning very differently at different ages, and their experience as learners is different at these ages. A system of levels that takes no account of these fundamental differences will not help teachers to help children.

This is compounded by the lack of coherence between the subjects and the fact that the criteria of assessment are not based on any educational research or evidence of what children can do at different ages or stages but merely what the subject working parties (mainly secondary subject specialists) thought. This is particularly damaging in the early years because the curriculum begins to be conceived in terms of complex concepts watered down rather than starting from what children already know from their first-hand experiences. This is very apparent with science where great anomalies exist. For example, at level 2 children are expected to 'give a simple account of the pattern of their own day' (SC AT 3, level 2) which is well within the grasp of most pre-school children, but also 'to be able to explain why night occurs' (SC AT 16, level 2) which would seem to involve many abstract concepts about the Earth in space which are outside the average seven-year-old's experiences.

Teachers are both overwhelmed and confused about what they are being asked to do within the National Curriculum. Teacher assessment is seen to be both formative and summative. Developments in teacher assessment have been emphasizing its formative role and the importance of more open recording systems to support this, but the assessments teachers are being asked to make are of children's levels on a ten-level continuum. Again, as Barrs says:

> . . . formative and summative assessment cannot easily draw on the same information because their needs are very different and, where there is a conflict, it will always be the needs of summative and evaluative assessment that prevail. This is in fact the case with the ten-level model itself which is far more suited to the needs of summative assessment, with its emphasis on numerical grades, than it is to the needs of formative assessment, which ought to be more detailed and qualitative in its description of progress.
>
> (Barrs, 1990, p. 45)

Teachers are being encouraged to continue to work on cross-curricular themes but are also being asked to assess subjects. They are being asked to provide evidence of their assessments of children's achievement in the attainment targets. For teachers at the end of key stage 1 this can mean assessing 35 attainment targets comprising over 200 statements of attainment. From even a cursory glance at the range of statements of attainment it is clear that there is tremendous range in the kind of things teachers are being asked to assess, many of which ask for 'knowledge and understanding'. These are notoriously difficult to assess unless over some lengthy period.

Also, as has been outlined in the first chapter, assessment has an expectation of accurate measurement in many teachers' eyes. There is a feeling that they are being asked to make accurate judgements about their pupils, and also that pupils are going to be graded on these assessments. This imposes a terrible burden of anxiety and responsibility on teachers, especially since the whole idea of equal opportunities in assessment seems to be ignored by the National Curriculum. These pressures are further compounded by the necessity for the teachers at the end of key stage 1 also to administer the SATs which will merely duplicate the work done by teacher assessment. As May Warris, head of a first school in Sheffield, said in *The Guardian* (2.4.91), 'The Government should rely on schools' own expertise in assessment. All the tests will do is check up on what the teachers are saying'.

The TGAT Report (DES, 1988a, para. 119) was aware of the problems of imposing a subject-based curriculum on primary schools and expecting them to assess it, and considered that 'there is still a potentially serious problem because of the size of the burden that could all too easily be placed on teachers in the primary phases'.

So it is not surprising that teachers feel themselves caught in an almost insoluble situation when they are trying to maintain formative assessment as part of good early years practice and yet are also trying to carry out their statutory responsibility to assess children's progress through the National Curriculum.

THE WAY FORWARD: TEACHER ASSESSMENT WITHIN THE NATIONAL CURRICULUM

The system that is currently in place is obviously at odds with the principles of assessing young children's learning. This final section will look at how it might be possible to move forward to ensure that the positive aspects of teacher assessment are not lost in the National Curriculum.

First, there is obviously the need for some re-assessment of the situation at key stage 1 to reduce the burden on the teachers. This should maintain teacher assessment as a way of monitoring children's progress and should provide guidance on record-keeping that is in line with the principles of teacher assessment outlined earlier.

A possible model of teacher assessment within the National Curriculum would include records of the content covered and linked to planning, and in-depth analysis of samples of children's work which would focus on the learning processes involved. These both need to be supplemented by records of teachers' relevant observations. Then the three need to be put together into a profile or record of achievement. These need to be considered in more detail.

Records linked to planning provide a record of what has been covered. Planning is an integral part of teaching and learning, and certainly part of good teaching. Teachers plan to ensure progression and balance in the curriculum, and will modify their plans in the light of their assessments and records. A generally accepted model of planning would consist of teachers' long-term plans for the class, supplemented by weekly and daily plans which make provision for groups and individual children. The long-term plans usually are based on the cross-curricular theme that the class is working on, and will mark the attainment targets covered. If teachers highlight the work actually covered the plans provide a record. Teachers' weekly and daily plans form a more useful form of record-keeping because they can be linked to groups of children and individual children, and provide better evidence for any summative record of what has been achieved.

Many teachers supplement their planning with tick-lists to show what individual children have covered. These may be kept by the teacher, or by the children, and may be cross-curricular or linked to one curriculum area. Checklists and tick-sheets are a well-established form of record-keeping and often seem the simplest, but they are really only a record of what has been achieved, a summative record. It is very difficult for checklists or tick-sheets to record the process of children's learning or for them to be used as a formative record. It is interesting to note that soon after the introduction of the National Curriculum many schools, LEAs and publishers evolved tick-sheets to record children's achievements in the National Curriculum, but it soon became apparent to those using them that they were not able to record adequately what children were doing.

What is needed is some form of record-keeping that allows the teacher to look in more detail at a piece of child's work, and to assess the content and the process. Teachers cannot possibly look at all work in this way but would focus on a *sample*. This idea of analysing samples of children's work is the most effective and useful form of assessment as it allows the teacher an in-depth snapshot view of the learning.

Sampling children's work is particularly suitable at key stage 1 when the learning process is crucial. It allows teachers to involve the children in the record-keeping by discussing with them what they were intending to do. This helps to clarify some of the misunderstandings between child and teacher over content and context mentioned in the previous section.

The samples of children's work can be original pieces or copies, and can be analysed during or after the event. The assessment can be recorded on a sheet attached to the sample. These samples need to be collected regularly but not often. They provide the evidence of children's progress and can include levels of achievement linked to the National Curriculum. Sampling also allows teachers to make cross-curricular assessments. The samples may be chosen by the teacher or the child and the child's comments also recorded. This is a way of recording and assessing endorsed by SEAC in the School Assessment Folder (SEAC, 1991). Certainly in order to assess adequately the process-orientated attainment targets in maths (ATs 1 and 8) and science (AT 1) teachers must sample children's work.

The assessments made from samples of children's work will need to be supplemented by *teachers' observations*. Observation is traditionally the strongest assessment tool of the early years teacher, because of the nature of young children's learning and the way early years classrooms are set up to facilitate this. The difficulty of observation is that it can be time consuming, particularly to record, and it requires teachers to know what is relevant to observe and record. For teachers at key stage 1 this means that they must have a good understanding of what is pertinent in children's development (and also of the National Curriculum). There will be certain stages in development that will be common to children at this stage and will need to be recorded, for example achieving on one-to-one correspondence in counting, or beginning to work collaboratively. These may or may not be relevant to the National Curriculum, but are important in terms of children's development. It will also be important to record observations that indicate children are moving on from an earlier assessment.

Observations must be a manageable part of assessment. They may be of class activities (for example, story time) or of individual children. They may be only for a matter of seconds, or for some minutes. Only relevant observations need to be recorded, otherwise the procedure gets out of hand. Sometimes teachers will have planned to observe a particular child or activity, at other times it will be quite random. Teachers need to be able to jot down their observations in a notebook in order to transfer them to a record later.

The records of children's work will build up over the year and will need to be organized and kept in some manageable way in the classroom. Many teachers have a file or scrapbook for each child, and keep these in the classroom. This allows the teacher and the child to add to them. At the end of the year they will need to be summarized into a *profile or record of achievement*. This can involve the child's and the parents' comments. It is a statutory part of the National Curriculum that parents receive annual reports on their child's progress in the National Curriculum, although it is only at the end of the key stage that these need to include the levels of attainment targets reached.

It is clear from this description of methods of record-keeping, that although it theoretically should be a manageable part of normal teaching, in practice it is complex and time consuming. The Primary Language Record and Primary Learning Record are able to meet these demands. Their strengths have already been outlined in a previous section, and this is a form of record that is able to take on the breadth of children's learning and addresses the issues of parental and child involvement, equal opportunities, bilingual pupils and children with special needs. As Barrs *et al.* note:

> The process of observing, noting and recording, with the support of a record like the Primary Language Record, helps to develop powers of observation, but also directs attention to what is significant in a child's behaviour. The framework present in the Record helps to structure these observations and provides the basis for a developing profile of a child's strengths and needs as a learner . . . [and] shows how the National Curriculum attainment statements can be fitted into this model of learning – which offers however a much

broader map of progress and development than the National Curriculum provides.

(Barrs *et al.*, 1990, p. 6)

Hopefully then teachers will be given encouragement to use educationally valid systems of assessment and record-keeping that are congruent with good early years practice. These systems need time to develop and evolve, and teachers need time to become familiar with processes of assessment and record-keeping that are holistic and formative. In the present climate there are doubts whether this will be possible.

SUMMARY AND CONCLUSIONS

Teacher assessment through record-keeping is of crucial importance as children make their way through the first years of schooling. It allows teachers to build up a picture of the child and use this to inform their future teaching.

Teacher assessments involve gathering evidence and making judgements about it. The criteria for making these judgements will reflect the assessors' view of learning. It is therefore important that the criteria used for assessing children at key stage 1 reflect a holistic and developmental view of learning.

During the last decade a more coherent body of work on teacher assessment has developed. This has established certain principles that should underpin teacher assessment and record-keeping. These principles establish that to be educationally valid teacher assessment and record-keeping should be a normal part of children's learning in the classroom and address the process and not merely the product of learning, and the children need to be clear about what is being assessed. In order to build up a broad picture of the child, all teachers who work with the child should contribute to the record, as should the child and the parents.

Despite the recognition of the importance of teacher assessment, there is a dearth of published materials that satisfy the principles outlined above. The Primary Language Record and the Primary Learning Record have been developed out of current thinking about teacher assessment, and take on the breadth of children's development.

The imposition of the National Curriculum and the statutory requirements for teacher assessment within it have undone much of the good work. No guidance has been given to teachers and there is a general feeling of panic.

Teacher assessment and record-keeping are complex and time consuming. The statutory requirements of teacher assessments and records of every statement of attainment by the end of the key stage may impose such an intolerable burden on teachers that they will be forced to abandon any in-depth analysis of pupils' work and resort to tick-sheets. Furthermore, despite being told that assessment should be the servant not the master, if the demands of teacher assessment are too great it will inevitably dominate the curriculum. Because the statements of attainment that teachers are being asked to assess are not the result of a coherent framework of learning but are isolated statements, teachers may be forced towards a system of teacher assessment that 'tests' the children for the statements of attainment rather than builds up a profile of children's progress and achievements. This goes against all the principles of educationally valid teacher assessment, and good early years practice. It is the teachers in the key stage 1 classes who will be trying to solve the dilemmas and contradictions of good practice and the demands of the National Curriculum.

It is of crucial importance that the burden of teacher assessment is limited and that the interrelationship between teacher assessment and the SATs at key stage 1 is clarified. This could be resolved by using teacher assessment only to assess children at key stage 1. If some form of moderation is introduced into those teacher assessments that relate to the National Curriculum, then some consistency would be ensured between teachers, schools and LEAs. This would make the SATs redundant and would leave some hope for the continuation of useful teacher assessment through record-keeping at key stage 1.

7
BILINGUALISM AND ASSESSMENT
Eve Gregory and Clare Kelly

The setting is an inner-city classroom of five- to six-year-olds. Husna and Naseema are reading Each, Peach, Pear, Plum, *by Janet and Allen Ahlberg, together. Despite the attractions of the illustrations, their eyes are drawn to the print and they read quickly and fluently. Husna points carefully to each word to help Naseema who is more hesitant. 'Each, Peach, Pear, Plum, I spy Tom Thumb. Tom Thumb in the cupboard, I spy Mother Hubbard. Mother Hubbard down the cellar, I spy Cinderella. Cinderella on the stairs, I spy the Three Bears . . .' Husna breaks off with 'I can count to ten in Bengali: Ek, dui, teen, chaar, panch, chhoy, shaat, aat, noy, dosh.' 'Gosh?' asks the teacher. 'Mmm. But this is ten/dosh, not like gosh in "Oh, my gosh, my golly." The teacher laughs, knowing she is referring to one of the 'Story-chest Big Books' with which she is very familiar. The children continue with the text glancing only occasionally at the illustrations which complement this nursery rhyme world. As they reach the page featuring a magnificent plum pie, the teacher interrupts and asks 'Can you show me the plum pie in that picture?' The children stare blankly at the teacher and the page. Eventually, Husna points quickly to something nondescript in the background. The teacher shows them the pie and allows the children to get back to their reading. They finish the text and are impatient to change the book for another.*

Like many of their class-mates, Husna and Naseema entered school speaking very little English. In just over a year, they will be examined on the same tests as their monolingual peers. Unlike children at school in Wales, who will be tested in spoken Welsh and receive teacher assessment only in their English reading skills, the Education Reform Act (1988) stipulates that all bilingual children in England must have equal access to the attainment targets and programmes of study of the National Curriculum and should be subject to the same tests. Annexe E of the Act allows exemption only for children who have been in Britain for less than six months.

The above interaction between two bilingual children and their teacher highlights a number of questions. What are the strengths and weaknesses of bilingual children after two or three years of school learning in a second language? Can these strengths and weaknesses be revealed adequately in tests designed for monolingual English seven-year-olds? What might be the dangers inherent in standardized tests? Should bilingual children be examined differently? Should the tests be in the children's first language? How far can monolingual teachers and testers be competent in assessing and testing bilinguals? Using the example of Husna, Naseema and their teacher as a springboard, this chapter aims to give the reader access to current research findings enabling informed answers to the above questions. Although the focus is on bilingual children, a number of issues are discussed which relate equally to the testing of all children whose cultural practices are not those of the white middle-class mainstream in British schools. Finally, if standardized tests were to be abandoned, what alternative approaches to assessing the progress of bilinguals might be developed for classroom use?

THE STRENGTHS AND WEAKNESSES OF BILINGUAL CHILDREN IN ENGLISH CLASSROOMS

As our above vignette shows Husna and Naseema reading, let us start by examining their likely performance on the SAT should it be administered to the children now. The attainments to be tested appear clear enough:

Level 1: Begin to recognize individual words or letters, such as shop signs or 'bus stop'; talk in simple terms about story content.
Level 2: Use pictures, context and phonic cues in reading; read something without help from the teacher and talk with confidence about it.
Level 3: Read familiar stories aloud with expression.

Testing Husna and Naseema, however, presents us with a dilemma. If we start at level 1, we find the children well able to recognize individual words and letters but often unable to talk about the story content, especially if it is new. However, if we jump to level 3, Husna, Naseema and their class-mates will have no difficulty in reading familiar stories out loud. But they will have considerable problems if presented with formal content-based questions to answer on them. The complexities involved in testing Husna and Naseema are already becoming apparent.

It is obvious that talking about the content of a story is going to be a much harsher test for children learning a second language than for their monolingual peers. If we take on board Sapir's claim that language 'does not . . . stand apart from or run parallel to direct experience but completely interpenetrates with it' (1970, p. 121) then we must recognize that bilingual children's performance will depend upon whether they can identify with the experience in English and consequently call upon appropriate lexis and structures with which to express it. During this learning process there is a considerable gap between what can be understood and what can be actively produced. Understanding cannot be examined by testing talk. Yet discussion and explanation are important attainment targets in all the core curriculum areas and have been picked out to be tested.

Level 2 gets to the heart of the reading process by testing how the children are progressing in making sense of print. It draws on recent research telling us that getting meaning from print means learning to utilize different cueing or 'clueing' systems to help predict the text (Goodman, 1973; Holdaway, 1979): semantic or meaning cues, where the reader has sufficient conceptual background and experience in the culture to make sense of what is being read; syntactic cues, where the reader is able to draw upon a knowledge of the grammatical structure of the language being read to predict correct parts of speech; and graphophonic cues, where a knowledge of sound/symbol associations helps accurate word prediction.

Most standardized reading tests for young children try to measure how competently these cueing systems are being used. Children are asked to complete sentences such as 'The p - - has run out of ink'. In the early stages help is often given in the form of a picture and/or choice of words e.g. plant, pen, elephant. Comprehension tests are also used to examine how far a child has understood a text. However, strict rules for ascertaining whether an answer is correct or wrong must be adhered to in order for a SAT to be standardized and summative. Any freedom of interpretation necessarily invalidates a test.

Husna and Naseema present us with a paradox. Strictly speaking, they are still unable efficiently to use any of these cues. Semantically, they do not yet have sufficient experience with English culture and language to predict likely objects or events. Syntactically, they often rely on repeating well-known 'formulae' (Hatch, Peck and Wagner-Gough, 1979) or whole chunks of speech or text as in 'Oh my gosh, my golly!'. Phonically, they are still sometimes unable to notice fine distinctions in sounds when meeting English words, for example 'dosh' and 'gosh'. Nor, of course, is their teacher as she encounters Bengali words. Sometimes it is difficult for the children to know what a sound actually refers to. Is a 'p' an object or a sound?

Yet their reading shows that Husna and Naseema are obviously taking meaning from print, which is the very first attainment target of key stage 1. But their way of coming to grips with a text is undoubtedly different from that of their monolingual peers. With time, they will be equally at home with all the cueing systems, but in this transitional stage other cues seem to be used in the quest for meaning. If bilingual children are showing evidence of learning differently from their monolingual peers, might we need a different way of measuring their progress and skills? But first, we need to be aware of what special linguistic, cognitive and social skills bilingual children bring with them in approaching the task of making sense of school learning.

Husna and Naseema's reading already provides evidence of a number of linguistic skills. They have completely separated their two languages and are able to use appropriate linguistic sets in different situations. They know the names of their two languages and refer to them. Moreover, they are learning to read not just in two languages, but using two totally different scripts. They have an interest and an excitement in the words themselves, shown by wanting to pick out individual words and compare them. They realize the arbitrary nature of language; that is, they know that words are not tied to their referents and that 'dosh' or 'gosh' can mean different things in different languages. This realization enabled an early mastery of one-to-one correspondence which we see now as they carefully point out separate words. The children show an awareness of the importance of syntax. They know that 'dosh' in Bengali is not just semantically different from the English, but is a different part of speech and must be used differently in sentences. From this, they realize that the syntax of a language is arbitrary too and can be different in different languages.

The awareness that language is arbitrary, together with a lack of knowledge of the conventional word, often enables the children to play with words and experiment with them. Teachers of bilingual children can provide lists of imaginative experiments with words such as 'a necklace man' (a mayor), 'a kissing lady' (a bride), 'Happy Wu Year' and 'a ghonster' (ghost monster). Lacking the conventional word used unconsciously by their monolingual peers forces these children into a conscious search for the real meaning behind a concept in order to find an appropriate synonym. These experiments show the children to be aware of what they do not know and to be active in devising various strategies to find out, such as asking 'What's the opposite of "up"?' In other words, they are using language to find out more about language itself.

The above examples all show the children to have what is called a highly developed metalinguistic awareness. This means that they are able to get outside language and be aware of its forms and properties (Baker, 1988) or to make language forms opaque and attend to them (Cazden, 1984). This type of knowledge found a strong place in English 5–16 (DES, 1984), Kingman (DES, 1988b) and English 5–11 (DES, 1988c). It is also in key stage 1 of the final orders. However, it does not feature in the attainment targets for SAT assessment.

Evidence for the linguistic strengths of bilingual children can be found in a number of studies. Vygotsky (1962, p. 110) claimed that bilingualism enabled a child 'to see his language as one particular system among many, to view its phenomena under more general categories . . . [which] leads to awareness of his linguistic operations'. Later work by Feldman and Shen (1971), Ianco-Worrall (1972), Ben-Zeev (1977), Swain and Cummins (1979), Bain and Yu (1980), Arnberg (1987) and Hakuta (1986), among others, has investigated different aspects of bilingual children's raised language consciousness and advanced metalinguistic skills. Some of this reflects closely strengths shown by Husna and Naseema and deserves further description.

Working with four- to nine-year-old monolingual English and bilingual Afrikaans/English children, Ianco-Worrall (1972) found that the bilinguals excelled in ability to state the principle that names are arbitrarily assigned to things. For example, they understood symbol substitution games such as the following two to three years earlier than their monolingual peers:

> Researcher: This is named 'plane', right?
> Well, in the game it's called turtle.
> Can the turtle fly?

Cummins (1978a) extended this in a test of fifty-three monolingual English and an equal number of bilingual English/Irish eight- to nine-year-olds, matched on verbal IQ, socio-economic group, sex and age. Here, children were not only asked whether words could be interchanged, but to justify their answers. A significantly higher number of bilingual children gave answers such as 'You could change the names because it doesn't matter what they are called', whereas a large majority of monolinguals replied 'They are their right names, so you can't change them'. Similar tests led the authors to conclude that bilingual children were better able to detect contradictions, ambiguities and tautologies and generally possess more flexibility and emancipation in separating words and their meanings.

Other studies have found evidence of a greater analytic ability of bilingual children. Ben-Zeev (1977) found that bilingual Hebrew/English children between five and eight were able not only to substitute nouns but to analyse linguistic stems by ignoring both word meaning and sentence framing, for example:

> Researcher: If 'they' means 'spaghetti', how do we say 'They are good children'?

In being able simultaneously to reply 'spaghetti are good children', the children had grasped the basic idea that the structure of language is different from the phonological representations and meaningful words in which it is embodied.

In a series of studies, Bialystok (1987) attempted to pinpoint exact linguistic operations in which bilingual children were more advanced than monolinguals. Advantage occurred when the children were (1) required to separate individual words from meaningful sentences, (2) focus on only the form or meaning of a word under highly distracting conditions, (3) reassign a familiar name to a new object. Each of these tasks requires selective attention to words or their features and the performance of some operation on an isolated component. The children's strength, therefore, may be to attend selectively to words and their boundaries. This is precisely what we see Husna and Naseema doing. Other studies have suggested that it may be the potential interference between the two languages as well as the incipient contrastive linguistics undertaken which force the child to make more processing effort (Baker, 1988). Such studies are important, as the supposed negative effects of interference have long been a strong argument for denying a child access to contrastive linguistics through bilingual education in the school setting.

These linguistic strengths stand in stark contrast with young bilingual children's performance in traditional language tests designed for monolingual children. When asked to re-tell a story, bilingual five-year-olds were found to make a far greater number of grammatical mistakes than their monolingual peers and were very inferior in the Peabody Picture Vocabulary Test in both their languages (Ben-Zeev, 1977). In other words, although their consciousness of language and their analytic skills were more advanced, they had less experience in each of their languages than their monolingual peers. The above studies begin to indicate both the untapped strengths of bilingual children and the biased nature of the SATs.

A number of studies argue that bilingual children have cognitive advantages over their monolingual peers. Husna and Naseema's ability to jump over semantic and syntactic boundaries with Husna's use of 'g/dosh' may be characteristic of what Ben-Zeev refers to as the 'liberated thought' of bilinguals. Their developing knowledge of different word and concept boundaries in different languages, for example the knowledge that 'cousin' is a broad-based concept in English, covering a number of different words and concepts in Bengali, may be an example of a 'cognitive flexibility' (Lambert, 1977). Through their developing bilingualism, the children are learning a double set of rules. These comprise not just the lexis and structure of a language but the boundaries of concepts and culture. Plum pies are not just words but a way of life.

Other studies have found bilingual children to be ahead in concept formation. This may take the form of an earlier ability to conserve measurement (Liedtke and Nelson, 1968), classify according to shape, colour or size (Ben-Zeev, 1977), or mentally manipulate and reorganize visual patterns (Peal and Lambert, 1962). From a number of tests, Peal and Lambert went on to conclude, '. . . there is no question about the fact that he (the bilingual child) is superior intellectually. In contrast, the monolingual appears to have a more unitary structure of intelligence, which he must use for all types of tasks' (p. 20).

The linguistic and cognitive advantages of bilingual children have often been attributed to their greater responsiveness to perceptual hints and clues than their monolingual peers. Ianco-Worrall (1972) and Ben-Zeev (1977) suggest that bilingual children have a greater social sensitivity. Their fear of falling into the wrong language makes them extra aware of the importance of appropriateness and they are constantly scanning to see if their language is correct. Other studies show bilingual children better able to adapt instructions to blindfolded children (Genesee, Tucker and Lambert, 1978) and more sensitive to facial expressions or other non-verbal communication (Bain and Yu, 1978; Skutnabb-Kangas, 1984). It was obvious to Husna and Naseema that the teacher did not share their language and they were keen to initiate her into it. Had she been more alert, she could have pointed out the difference in the sound of 'dosh' and 'gosh'. As it was, the children gave her their own feedback on the different use of the word.

The above studies end this section with a paradox: if bilingual children are linguistically, cognitively and socially advantaged, why do many fall behind in school? We read that Bangladeshi children particularly suffer 'severe educational underachievement' (Home Affairs Committee,

1986/7). Two main explanations have been offered in research studies. First, bilingualism must be additive not subtractive in order for the advantages outlined above to ensue. This means that a second language and culture must be added to the first and not replace them (Cummins, 1978b, Swain and Cummins, 1979). Second, the child's first language must be of high and not low prestige (Skutnabb-Kangas, 1984). Both of these factors demand that a child's existing linguistic competence be recognized. If bilingual children are being examined on tests written by monolinguals for monolinguals using material which only monocultural children can identify with, none of these potential strengths will be revealed. To understand more fully the dangers of such tests, we need to examine past experiences from both home and abroad.

STANDARDIZED TESTS AND BILINGUAL CHILDREN: LESSONS FROM HOME AND ABROAD

> . . . the number of aliens deported because of feeble-mindedness . . . increased approximately 350% in 1913 and 570% in 1914. This was due to the untiring efforts of the physicians who were inspired by the belief that mental tests could be used for the detection of feeble-minded aliens . . .
>
> (Goddard, 1917)

It is easy now to react with incredulity at such a belief. Official prejudice based on this level of naivety appears unthinkable today. However, a moment's pause forces us to ask how far the belief has really disappeared or whether it is simply expressed in a more subtle form. With this question in mind, the section which follows investigates tests which have been given to young children who are still 'strangers' to the language and culture of the classroom. We begin by examining briefly the nature of bias in standardized tests and ways in which this reflects in minority group children's test results. We then review briefly lessons which have been learned from tests in the United States and Canada. Finally, we relate these experiences to the situation in British infant schools and consider what questions remain unanswered. Such terms as 'feeble-minded' may no longer be used, but will children's bilingualism mean they are still seen as 'slow learners'? Is it possible to test a young bilingual's real ability in school?

Nearly a century later, it appears obvious that the real issue behind the 'feeble-minded aliens' in the quotation above was socio-political. The aim was to restrict entry to foreigners who could not speak English while at the same time maintaining they were being given a 'fair' test. Cummins (1984) argues that school tests today serve similar socio-political aims which militate against the success of minority group children. He illustrates how standardized tests, especially verbal ones, must inevitably be biased against minority groups. By definition, the standardization of a test on a representative sample means that the bulk of the sample will come from the dominant group. Individual minority groups will only be represented to a minor extent. Thus, in the pilot stage of item development, the majority of items selected for try-out will reflect the prior learning experiences of the majority Anglo group.

For Husna and Naseema in our last section, this means that even if items reflecting their unique learning experiences were to be included in the try-out phase, they would be quickly screened out in the final item analysis. The very nature of 'standardization' means the inclusion only of items which are neither too easy nor too difficult for the majority of children. Husna and Naseema's linguistic skills would be too advanced for the majority of the test norming sample and would, therefore, not correlate well with the total test. In this way, standardized tests are 'culture loaded' (Kaufman, 1979) to reflect both the language and values of the dominant group. This demonstrates that, as we saw in Chapter 1, they are norm-referenced in spite of every claim that they should be criterion-referenced.

The 'culture loading' of standardized tests needs further explanation. How can, for example, describing a scientific process, discussing a story or working with two- and three-dimensional shapes (all attainment targets to be covered by the SATs) reflect anything but what the child has learned in school?

Ethnographic studies which follow the child from home into school provide a number of examples showing how the socialization or learning experiences of minority groups may differ in many respects from those of the dominant Anglo group. Heath's study (1983) of two working-class communities living only a few miles apart in the Appalachians shows how each group differs greatly in ways of socializing children. From data collected over ten years, Heath argues that even what counts as an acceptable 'story' is culturally determined. The religious demands of the white community cause their children to find difficulty in responding to any story which is not 'true'. The other group has equal difficulty in keeping within the boundaries of 'truth' for news-time presentations.

The actual way events are narrated also differs according to cultural background. In a study of infant children's 'news retellings' in the United States, Michaels (1986) shows how Anglo-American children have very different discourse styles from the Afro-American minority group. The majority children use what she refers to as a 'topic-centred' approach where talk focuses on one particular topic, whereas the minority children's talk is 'topic-associating' where a number of topics radiate from an initial theme. In a standardized test, only one approach, i.e. that of the majority group, could score as logical.

Michaels argues that if children's contributions are treated differentially, they may well refuse to answer the teacher at all. Her conclusions are backed up by ethnographic evidence indicating, as we saw in Chapter 2, that a child's willingness to respond at all to a test is strongly influenced by whether cultural norms from home correspond or clash with those in school. Phillips' (1972) seminal study on the native American-Indian children of Warm Springs was the first of a number showing how children's apparent refusal to join in lessons can be attributed to the fundamental disparity of participatory norms between home and school. Guthrie and Hall (1983) refer to such differences as a basic 'cultural mismatch' between home and school which will be reflected in children's school performance.

Children's response to words themselves will differ according to the frequency with which they have been encountered. The cross-cultural psychologist Michael Cole (1975, pp. 51–2) points out that 'children from different sub-cultural groups are exposed to different vocabulary. How children (or adults) respond to a problem (even one so simple as saying what comes to mind when we say "peach") depends in large measure on their familiarity with the content of the problem and this familiarity varies in unknown ways with the child's home culture'.

The French equivalent of the reading SAT for seven-year-olds may provide a window into this. The task is to select the correct words in a passage about 'father is an ogre' (papa est un ogre): 'Mon père, lui, c'est (difficile/différent) c'est un (ogre/orgue). Aujourd'hui mes copains viennent (jour/jouer) chez moi. De la fenêtre de la cuisine, papa les (guette/guêpe) "Le petit sera mon hors d'oeuvre, le gros le plât de resistance, et le maigre mon (désert/dessert)".' The problem for a French–Arabic bilingual child is not just one of language. Success demands both the willingness to suspend reality and a familiarity with European eating habits. We are reminded here of Husna, Naseema and their teacher's reaction to the 'plum pie' in the last section.

One analysis of an actual standardized test begins to detail more precisely the possible effects of the home culture upon a child's performance. Using examples which closely reflect those of Husna and Naseema, Ribeiro (1980) records how Portuguese children in the United States easily manage some advanced test questions such as 'What is the meaning of "migrate"?' and 'Why does oil float on water?' 'Migrate' is an important word in the lives of their families and all the children are familiar with seeing oil float on water from the lamp near the altar in the Catholic church. On the other hand, the 'easier' question 'Why are cats and mice alike?' (Answer: they are both animals) is extremely difficult, for cats and mice are seen rather in terms of their *different* functions than by their similarity, i.e. the mouse is a nuisance because it devours grain whereas the cat is useful for eating the mouse. Ribeiro argues, too, that tests involving abstract shapes and three-dimensional blocks make greater demands upon those who have no such toys at home.

The above instances show how certain standardized test items will make sense to some children but not others. Donaldson (1978) has demonstrated how very young children are capable of relatively complex operations when a task is presented in a context which is familiar and makes 'human sense'. We must presume, therefore, that familiarity is likely to make a crucial difference in children's examination performance. For example, in a test of 100 vocabulary items used in Afro-American slang, Williams (1975) found that a black high school group averaged 36 points higher than the white. Standardized tests which focus on a limited sample of children's knowledge of Anglo-oriented tasks have, therefore, been held up as biased and restricted in their results.

Minority group parents in Canada and the United States who have campaigned for the educational rights of their children are by no means unaware of this bias. Official response in the two countries has, however, been very different. In the United States changes have resulted from litigation. In the 1970 Diana versus State Board of Education case, nine Mexican–American children who had been placed in special education classes on the basis of verbal tests gained the provision that 'all children whose home language is other than English must be tested in both their primary language and English . . . such children must be tested only with tests or sections of tests that do not depend on such things as vocabulary, general information and other similarly unfair verbal questions'. The Education of All Handicapped Children Act in 1975 stipulated further that tests must not be culturally discriminating. In Canada, change has rather been instigated by school boards concerned with multiculturalism. The York Board of Education in Toronto, for example, stipulates that 'linguistic and cultural factors will render results of such (academic) tests meaningless in the case of immigrant students and these results, if recorded in the student's records, can have an adverse influence on the student's academic progress . . . immigrant students should be excluded from such mass testing during their first two years in Canada'.

Responses in both Canada and the United States give bilingual children more rights than they at present have in Britain. However, both leave a number of questions untouched. Is a culturally undiscriminating test possible? While tests are standardized on the majority group and until all children share the same cultural background, the answer suggests not. Are two years in a country long enough to guarantee equality with monolingual children? Cummins (1984) suggests that a child needs five to six years to gain parity in English with a monolingual child on every level.

Finally: is it adequate to test a child in his/her first language? A return to Sapir and the body of research mentioned in the last section arguing for an intimate link between language and experience reveals the complexity of this question. If a curriculum is being taught only in English, it is highly unlikely that the appropriate specialist vocabulary will be accessible to a child in the first language. The story language of plum pies, the scientific lexis involved in describing the workings of a water pump or even talking about odd and even numbers may well not be within a child's first language experience. Only children following a parallel syllabus in the first language at home or at an evening or Saturday class would benefit from first language testing. The conclusion, therefore, that it would be fairer to examine a bilingual child in the first language is potentially a very dangerous one. We cannot suppose that a complex and specialist vocabulary will be available in a young child's first language simply because it is lacking in the second. Results from first language tests are likely to strengthen the belief that bilinguals may be 'slow learners' or, to return to the quotation opening this section, 'feeble-minded'.

Responses from the United States and Canada both overlook the fundamental question: how can standardized tests give a true insight into a child's knowledge and potential? If we maintain that this is our ultimate aim as teachers then we shall need to look beyond the results of SATs whether conducted in a child's first or second language.

ISSUES OF PEDAGOGY AND TEACHER ASSESSMENT – THE WAY FORWARD?

All pupils share the same statutory entitlement to a broad and balanced curriculum, including access to the National Curriculum.
(DES, 1989a, para. 8:1)

The above statement may at first appear uncontentious, but the question is, does it go far enough for children like Husna and Naseema whom we met at the beginning of this chapter? They should be offered not merely equality of entitlement to participate in the National Curriculum but an equal opportunity to succeed, to achieve. This section addresses issues of pedagogy and assessment and focuses on how linguistic and cultural differences can be viewed in positive terms both cognitively and socially within a teacher-led assessment framework which recognizes and encourages the creative nature of second language learning.

Significant developments have been made in recognizing and meeting the needs of second language learners since the Bullock Report declared 'no child should be expected to cast off the language and culture of the home as he crosses the school threshold' (DES, 1975, p. 543). In the current climate, however, such developments are in danger of being lost because teachers are feeling increasingly constrained by the limits of attainment targets and standardized tests and the rhetoric of the National Curriculum, which pays lip-service to the competences of second language learners (DES, 1990a) but in its reports presents no suggestions for facilitating their learning as opposed to testing their acquisition of skills and knowledge.

As we have seen in the previous section, such tests do not allow for cultural differences and assume that those being tested form one homogeneous group. They assess aptitudes regarded as intelligent within the dominant group and exclude any culturally specific ways in which children have learned to be intelligent (Brice Heath, 1983). Furthermore, children's developing understanding is underestimated when their cognitive functioning is assessed through the medium of a language in which they have had insufficient time to acquire proficiency. In short, summative assessment under the National Curriculum serves to marginalize further an already vulnerable group by focusing on conventional measures of skills and knowledge and failing to reveal the particular strengths and abilities that minority group children bring to the learning task.

Clearly, teacher assessment is the tool which should be used to provide 'rounded qualitative judgements' (DES, 1989a, para. 6:5) and offers the opportunity for the personal and intellectual growth of all learners to be recognized and recorded. The Education Reform Act (1988) assures us that teachers are free to employ their own methods of formative assessment, yet there is a disturbing tendency, as we saw in Chapter 2, for teachers to use the summative measures (attainment targets) as a yardstick for formative assessment and recording (Barrs, 1990), thereby losing their valuable opportunities to use their skills and professional judgement in a way that will be of great benefit to children and their families, particularly those from bilingual communities.

It would seem that there is a place for a philosophy of bilingual education to be debated publicly amongst the teaching profession, a debate that would consider total educational experience, and which would not only continue to explore the place of bilingualism in children's intellectual, social and cultural development but more crucially would address the issue of how teachers can move forward effectively in assessing the achievements of second language learners and documenting their progress.

Since the assessment process 'needs to be incorporated systematically into teaching strategies and practices at all levels' (DES, 1988a, para. 4), it is appropriate here to focus on the extent to which pedagogy can alleviate the cultural mismatch experienced by many minority children and the consequent effect upon their intellectual and personal development. Research (McDermott, 1978; Mohatt and Erickson, 1981) has shown the extent to which children are unable to participate in classroom life when the interactional style demanded by a teacher from the dominant group differs significantly from that of the minority culture.

In 1971 the KEEP project (Kamehameha Early Education Program) in America demonstrated clearly how academic achievement is directly related to the experiences to which children are exposed. The project was set up to improve the low performance of native Creole-speaking Hawaiian children who were inattentive, uninvolved and often aggressive in class. Ethnographic studies showed that in their communities, the same children were used to little adult supervision, worked co-operatively, and their learning was based on observing other children. When the restrictive culturally specific participant structures (Phillips, 1972) were uncovered and classroom communication and management structures were revised in line with the children's familiar cultural practices, they experienced an increase in motivation and consequent rise in academic achievements. It must be said, however, that ethnographic researchers in the KEEP project worked for many years to uncover the exact patterns of communication that were impeding children's development; nevertheless this project and others (Phillips, 1972; Fillmore, 1983; Heath, 1983) show clearly that underachievement is caused by the inadequacy of classroom practices to meet the child's needs rather than by the incompetence of the child.

As educationists we need to examine our practice and reassess the linguistic and cultural assumptions on which it is based, and move forward to accommodate what Heath (1983) characterizes as different ways of talking and knowing which will benefit all students. It becomes very important therefore to gain insights into the learning experiences of the minority child within his or her community. At the same time we must recognize the huge demands this will make upon a teacher whose class members represent a variety of groups and sub-groups. Parents and other members of the community who are willing to allow their language skills to be used as a resource have a major role to play in acquainting staff with the linguistic and cultural background of the children in their care.

It can be seen therefore that the emphasis must be on establishing appropriate patterns of communication within the classroom which will allow both the facilitation and the assessment of linguistic, cognitive and social skills. The importance of an interactional framework within which the children are encouraged to collaborate with their peers or a sympathetic adult in situations which hold real meaning for them has already been indicated. Such research suggests that heuristic approaches to learning that emphasize the importance of co-operation are successful for learning a second language (Fillmore, 1983; Krashen, 1981), developing an understanding of cultural and linguistic variety (Barnes, 1976) and promoting higher level thinking (Wells, 1986; Vygotsky, 1978). Clearly, accurately assessing the understanding gained by second language learners in any of these areas is problematic, even if qualitative, non-criterion-referenced models of teacher assessment are developed. This is undoubtedly one of the reasons why, despite the existence of enlightened policies in the United States and Canada, there are still no empirically supported alternative assessment procedures for minority children (Cummins, 1984).

Any system of formative assessment would need to recognize and incorporate three distinct areas which are of particular significance to second language learners and which do not feature in the standardized measures:

(1) The sophisticated linguistic skills required for the code switching and spontaneous translation which is a common feature of most multilingual classrooms.
(2) The existing conceptual understanding of a child who may not as yet have gained the linguistic facility to give it expression in a new language.
(3) The developing ability of the child to acquire a new language and use it in a creative way for his or her own purposes even at the earliest stages.

The following section will examine each of these areas in turn and attempt to suggest ways in which they can be incorporated into on-going teacher assessment.

Any system of assessment that recognizes and attempts to build upon the metalinguistic awareness of young second language learners and their ability to understand the symbolic and abstract nature of language would need to be grounded in what Marie Clay refers to as 'systematic observation of learning' (Clay, 1979). Such observation would necessarily be based upon the teacher's clear understanding of the development of linguistic skills and knowledge of the wider context in which children learn, and would be formalized in a record-keeping system that adopted a broad view of achievement similar to that embodied in the Primary Learning Record (CLPE, 1990a). In this way the considerable capabilities of children like Husna and Naseema would be acknowledged.

Children who come to this country with a well-developed conceptual framework but need time (more than the six months allowed under the National Curriculum) to develop the linguistic proficiency necessary to explain complex ideas successfully, require a system of teaching and assessment that will both help them to attain that proficiency and allow them to show what they really know. Cummins (1984) suggests that providing second language learners at all levels with tasks that are both cognitively demanding and yet firmly embedded in context, ensures a more successful communication of ideas, since learners will be able to rely on a wide range of situational cues in order to negotiate meaning. Although good early years practice recognizes the importance of meaningful contexts for all learning, it must be acknowledged, too, that there are particular benefits for second language learners since they will be supported in what Cummins refers to as 'surface fluency'. Such surface fluency, he argues, is necessary for basic interpersonal communicative skills (BICS), and at the same time provides a basis for the acquisition of academically related aspects of language necessary for cognitive academic language proficiency (CALP) and upon which learners can build as they extend their conceptual understanding.

The provision of context-embedded, cognitively demanding tasks will ensure a higher degree of success in facilitating and assessing children's learning (Donaldson, 1978). Such tasks should enable children to develop a more positive self-image when faced with the challenging task of becoming proficient in a second language, whilst building on the cognitive gains achieved in the first.

Any assessment of language acquisition would need to take account of the notion that language learning is an untidy process and as such presents many problems for formulating evaluative procedures.

Fillmore (1976) has suggested that a child in a natural environment will go through three stages in acquiring a second language. First, she or he will establish social relationships with speakers of the second language and in doing so will rely heavily on both non-verbal communication and fixed verbal formulae. Moving on to the second stage, she or he will begin to generate meaning by using new combinations of the formulaic words and finally will concentrate on the correctness of language form itself. Fillmore has identified five cognitive strategies employed during these stages. Such strategies could form the basis of a system for both assessing progress in each area and also evaluating the performance of teachers in scaffolding children's achievement in language.

The first of these strategies is to assume that what people are saying is directly relevant to the situation at hand or to what they or you are experiencing – their metastrategy being to guess. Teachers would need to evaluate how far what they are saying is relevant to context and, as discussed earlier, ensure situational, non-verbal cues to support communication.

The second strategy is to get some expressions that are understood and start talking; the third is to look for recurring parts in formulae. Teachers would need to be aware of which formulae are available to children and examine ways in which to facilitate children's language development by encouraging them to talk, thereby using and building upon the fixed formulae.

The fourth strategy is to make the most of what is available; and the fifth to work on 'big things', saving the details for later. Teachers would need to ensure that children were operating in a context that enabled them both to use formulae with which they were familiar and at the same time take the risks necessary to work on the 'big things' and in doing so arrive at a clearer understanding of how language works.

Fillmore further suggests that second language learners employ three social strategies in order to support their own learning:

(1) Join a group and act as if you understand what is going on, even if you don't.
(2) Give the impression with a few well-chosen words that you can speak the language.
(3) Count on your friends for help.

Teachers would need to examine the extent to which second language learners are given the opportunities to develop social relationships and operate within an environment where they are enabled through their own motivation to employ such strategies in an uninhibited way.

This section, which has focused on teacher-led assessment, has shown that in order for young minority group learners to be assessed fairly, teachers need first to understand the principles of language development and second to be aware of the social and educational factors that shape it. Above all, we must not lose sight of the importance of what Vygotsky

(1978) has termed the 'zone of proximal development' and the key role played by teachers and others in helping the child's 'ripening structures' to develop and the significance of such practice in any teacher-led assessment procedure.

SUMMARY AND CONCLUSIONS

In this chapter, we have examined some of the implications of assessment by testing for bilingual and minority group children. We have argued that standardized tests are, by their very nature, biased against minority groups. Finally, we have given examples of formative assessment which take into account a child's linguistic and cultural background. These offer the teacher methods of both analysing and developing children's individual language learning strategies in the classroom.

Examples from Europe and the United States reveal the dangers inherent in using evidence from standardized tests to draw conclusions on the conceptual or linguistic competence of minority groups. The dangers are both personal and political: personal in that a child's bilingualism is marginalized and language is viewed only in terms of 'English'; political in that the publication of 'official' test scores may lead to a 'ghettoization' of schools with a high intake of minority group children. The term 'English' in the National Curriculum is itself significant. Despite the fact that 70 per cent of the world population speaks more than one language and bi- or trilingualism is, therefore, normal (Marland, 1987), the statutory guidelines state that children should receive bilingual teaching support 'only until such time as they are competent in English' (DES, 1988b, para. 10:10). The National Curriculum for Wales recommends the teaching of Welsh and recognizes the advantages of bilingualism in extending social and cultural choice. These choices, however, are not extended to children in England.

Husna and Naseema have language learning strategies which reveal a very different competence from that of a monolingual six-year-old. Their competence is rooted in an acute awareness of language as a system rather than a knowledge of English as one particular system. Such competence is strongly recommended in both the Kingman (DES, 1988b) and Cox Reports (DES, 1988c), yet it receives no place in the English SATs. Language awareness, therefore, is seen as valuable only in so far as it is useful in improving a child's actual performance in English. Perera (1988) aptly parodies this 'usefulness' approach when she quotes Bloor (1979) who asks: 'Should we tell biology teachers they should not teach their pupils about the digestive system unless they can prove that doing so enables them to digest their food better?' Language, she argues, is an integral and fascinating part of our environment – every bit as important as the electric bell or the Spinning Jenny.

The present National Curriculum implies that Husna and Naseema's nascent bilingualism is just one stage along the path to monolingual fluency. This subtractive model of language learning is fuelled by commonsense notions that developing proficiency in a first language will interfere with conceptual development or acquisition of a second. Research highlighted in this chapter shows clearly how beneficial bilingualism may be. But for this to occur, appropriate teaching and assessment strategies must be devised, underpinned by a sound knowledge of the complex interplay of language and culture in a child's school learning. An essential part of this is a recognition of the role of bilingualism in promoting cognitive and linguistic growth. We are told that education is to develop the child as 'a future adult member of the community' (DES, 1989b, para. 2.2). How far that future community is successfully multicultural and multilingual will lie ultimately in the hands of those devising the National Curriculum and its tests.

8
IN CONCLUSION

Geva Blenkin and Vic Kelly

This brief concluding chapter seeks to identify and pull out the major themes which have permeated all the earlier chapters of this book, and to set them in the context of current practices and policies within the National Curriculum testing programme. In doing so, it will confront, or at least highlight, the political realities of that programme and raise the question of whether it is consistent with its own stated aim of raising educational standards.

Three main themes have emerged from all of the contributions to this book's exploration of assessment in the early years, no matter from what angle the issues have been viewed or approached. First, there is a clear recognition of the need for assessment in education and of the necessity of interweaving that assessment appropriately and effectively with curricular provision. Second, it has become very plain that, to meet these demands, highly sophisticated forms of assessment must be, and for some time now have been, devised. And third, there is the manifest evidence that the forms of testing, external and standardized, which are currently being imposed on pupils in the early years of their education fall far short of that level of sophistication.

None of this will of course come as a surprise to anyone who has been a student of education during recent years. For such a person will be well aware of the increasing importance that assessment has been seen to assume during that time, the developing recognition of the complexities of the relationship between assessment and curriculum, and the emergence of complex, subtle and sophisticated forms of assessment, such as Records of Achievement, which mirror the complexities of that relationship, and indeed of the concepts of assessment and curriculum themselves. These forms have recognized that educational assessment is a matter of judgement rather than of measurement; that such judgements can be properly

163

made only by those who know the children – teachers, parents and others who work closely with them; that, while it must undoubtedly at some stage – but surely not at six or seven – attempt to provide some kind of certification with national validity, its main, indeed its only *educational* justification or *raison d'être* is its contribution to the continuing development of the pupil; that it must thus be formative in both its intention and its effects; that to achieve this it must seek to identify strengths to be built on rather than weaknesses and inadequacies to be advertised; and that, to be supportive of development and to reflect the realities of that form of human development we call education, it must seek to assess achievement holistically rather than incrementally or by attempting to aggregate 'measurements' of a series of discrete and unconnected aspects of performance.

That same student of education will also be aware that in parallel with these developments in our understanding of the purposes, the nature and the practice of educational assessment, indeed in opposition to those developments, recent years have also seen the imposition of forms of assessment which fall far short of reflecting those principles, and owe more to political expediency and a desire to reduce expenditure on education than to any genuine concern for educational planning or the quality of provision. Thus these forms have stressed the metric rather than the judgemental, the summative rather than the formative, the incremental aggregation of 'scores' rather than holistic assessment, and thus attainment rather than development. They have sought for simplistic forms of assessment rather than recognizing or acknowledging its complexities. They have ignored the integral relationship of assessment and curriculum to the point of planning the assessment programme (through the TGAT group) before considering curriculum provision, and creating two quite separate bodies charged with the separate planning and administration of each. And they have insisted on propounding the myth, or maintaining the folklore, that short, externally created and administered tests will offer more reliable information about pupil progress than the comments and insights of those who work with these pupils every day. In short, they have failed to distinguish testing and assessment, both conceptually and practically.

It is important to recognize that different systems of assessment must be adopted to serve different purposes. One of the most common errors that has been made in the development of assessment schemes, and not only in the National Curriculum scheme, is that of assuming that one form or system of assessment can meet all the many different demands that may be made of it. It really is a nonsense – or perhaps merely the worst kind of idealistic wishful thinking – to claim, as we saw in Chapter 1 it has been claimed (DES, 1989b), that assessment must at every stage be formative, summative, evaluative, informative and helpful for professional development. This kind of 'pie-in-the-sky' approach is unhelpful to practitioners not only because it is conceptually muddled but also because it is silly and wrong. At best it is an example of the rhetoric which we are increasingly used to having directed at us by government agencies, including HMI. The TGAT Report itself (DES, 1988a, para. 13), as we also saw in Chapter 1, drew our attention to the fact that 'no system has yet been constructed that meets all the criteria of *progression, moderation, formative,* and *criterion-referenced* assessment' (let alone summative, evaluative, informative and helpful for professional development too). And it was suggested there that it is at least as likely that the failure to devise such a system is due to its total impossibility as to any lack of ingenuity on the part of those engaged in earlier attempts at developing assessment systems.

If different forms of assessment are needed, to meet different assessment goals and purposes, then, conversely, the forms chosen must reflect the goals and purposes of those who choose them. We have throughout this book advocated those forms we consider are most conducive to the promotion of educational growth in pupils – those which are formative, holistic, emphasizing strengths rather than weaknesses, judgemental rather than metric and so on. If we were right to make this claim, then to reject those forms and adopt others must imply and reveal a completely different set of goals and purposes. To go further than that and to advocate and implement not an alternative form of assessment but simple testing procedures is to declare even more plainly that one's goals and purposes are not educational in any sense of the term.

What, then, might the purposes of such a system of testing be? They can only be political. Their stated aims may be the raising of standards but again this must be recognized as rhetoric in the light of the realities of the testing system which is being created and imposed.

For that system is built on several assumptions. First, it is built on the assumption that educational standards are falling, although there is no concrete evidence for this empirical assertion. Nor is this only an assumption; it is constantly being asserted by politicians and others. To make such a claim without evidence is at best mischievous and irresponsible; at worst it is a device which is often used by politicians to gain their own ends, the device of 'rubbishing' the opposition and demeaning their discourse, in this case the concepts of education, curriculum, assessment, standards and development which form the professional framework of theory within which most teachers carry out their professional tasks.

A further assumption is that teachers' judgements and teachers' assessments are not to be trusted. This too is often asserted publicly. Again there is no evidence to support this claim. In fact, such evidence as there is points to teacher assessments being at least as accurate and fair as the most carefully standardized tests. And certainly, as we have seen, they can be holistic, formative, sympathetic to both the strengths and weaknesses of pupils, and productive in curricular terms, in a way that no standardized test could ever hope to be. Therefore, we can only assume that the purpose of making this kind of unsupported assertion and of developing a system of testing which emphasizes the – as yet undemonstrated – superior validity and reliability of standardized tests is not to enhance the quality of educational provision but to achieve ends of a political kind.

Third, it is assumed, and again asserted publicly, that these tests provide an objective measurement of pupils' attainment. However, we have seen that there is no evidence to support this and that, in fact, all the evidence there is points to the inaccuracy and unreliability of this form of testing. One cannot even say that it is inaccurate and unreliable in a fair and impartial way, since this kind of testing, again as we have seen, discriminates quite unfairly against certain kinds of pupil, especially the bilingual pupils which were the subject of Chapter 7, and in favour of others. To continue to assert the merits of this kind of test, when such a claim is manifestly unsupported, and indeed contradicted, by the evidence, again indicates that the goals of the system are political rather than educational, and that they are in reality very different from those stated.

What, then, are the political goals of current policies? What could be the point of publicly making false claims and accusations of this kind? First, as we noted in Chapter 1, they are designed to wrest control of the curriculum from the hands of teachers and local education authorities, and place it in the hands of central government. This of course is the prime purpose of the National Curriculum. However, the only effective means of enforcing the implementation of that curriculum in every detail is to test pupils regularly on their progress through it – not to assist their progress but rather to ensure that their schools and teachers do not devote too much of their time and attention to any other forms of learning. The testing system is thus primarily a device for ensuring that every aspect of the National Curriculum is taught – and taught effectively. In itself, this system contributes nothing to the raising of standards, however these are defined, and it may indeed operate against that process. Only if the National Curriculum itself is raising standards can the testing programme devised to impose it on schools be justified in the same terms – and then only if it can be shown that it is not working against it. The testing programme thus has no merits in itself.

Second, little secret has been made of the fact that the programme is also intended to provide the data on which individual schools and individual teachers can be appraised and made fully accountable for their work. For the results of these tests must by law be published at key stages 2, 3 and 4; and it has been strongly recommended by the Secretary of State that they be published at key stage 1 too. (The fact that publication is not required by law at this key stage must indicate doubts on the part of the authors of the system of its worth, validity and justification at this stage.) Even if one ignores questions of the morality of using data of such manifest inaccuracy for purposes such as this, it must be noted that such tests offer a very limited view of what schools are doing and imply a comparably limited view of what schools, and indeed education, are for. They tell us nothing about what a school may be doing to promote the development of its pupils along the many dimensions of development other than the academic or intellectual. And they make no allowance for the significant differences in the circumstances in which schools are operating – the particular challenges facing schools in inner-city areas, for example. Even as a device for teacher or school appraisal and accountability, therefore, the system is crude, fundamentally inaccurate, unhelpful and unfair.

Third, when one asks why such a flawed system is being implemented, the only reasonable answer one can come up with (since it is unproductive and disturbing to explain it in terms of the fact that we may be being ruled by people who are either mad or of extremely low intellectual calibre) is that its underlying goal and purpose is to reduce public expenditure on education. This may seem an odd conclusion to reach when one considers how many millions of pounds have been spent – perhaps one should say wasted – on the production of SATs and the implementation of the testing system, not to mention the massive supporting documentation with which we are bombarded almost daily. In the long term, however, this would seem to be the only real point and purpose of the exercise. And in support of that conclusion, one might point out that the 1988 Education Act, along with its National Curriculum and its assessment programme, is the culmination of a consistent policy of centralization of control – pursued one might add, by both Conservative and Labour governments – which began with, or at least was given major impetus by, the economic problems which followed the oil crisis of 1974. The creation of a proper education service, which will genuinely serve the needs of all pupils, regardless of social or ethnic background or of natural ability, in short the provision of a proper 'entitlement curriculum', requires a unit of resource – at all levels, including that of higher education – considerably greater than that which is currently being made available. The only way in which any government can make a lesser provision and at the same time retain its credibility is by blaming the teaching profession for its previous 'prodigality' with resources and by creating a system of control which will enable it to keep all heads of expenditure to a minimum. Teachers, schools and, indeed, local authorities, would spend far more on educational provision, in an attempt to meet a much wider ranging set of perceived needs, than central government is prepared to spend. Their concept of educational need must therefore be restricted – by publicly rubbishing that concept as the product of woolly-minded educational idealists and/or 'loony-left' local authorities and by the implementation of a much more narrowly conceived National Curriculum, and their attention must be focused on this restricted form of provision – by a nationally controlled and administered testing system.

We must finally assert, therefore, that these political goals are being achieved, if they are indeed being achieved, at a cost. That cost is the negative impact that the testing programme must have, and that we can already see it is having, on the quality of the educational experiences now being made available to pupils at all stages, but especially in the early years. A narrow concept of education, as the acquisition of knowledge in a limited range of school subjects, allied to a traditional and Eurocentric definition of those subjects, must lead to disadvantages and deficiencies in the provision made for the many pupils for whom this form of provision may not be the most suitable form of educational diet, and by association for all pupils. And a testing system designed to maintain and reinforce that narrow form of curriculum must lead to a diminution of the experiences that can be offered to all pupils. That is the essence of an assessment-led or, worse, a test-led, curriculum. Pupils are offered, and can only be offered, that which the tests emphasize. And that, increasingly, is a very limited fare indeed.

For the realities of the testing programme are beginning to emerge as it is implemented for the first time at key stage 1. Indeed, the picture changes, or at least develops, daily. Books cannot be written as fast as Secretaries of State can be changed or as fast as policies change with them. Nor can complex debates of the kind this book has attempted to unfold be adapted sufficiently rapidly to keep up with the careering progress towards the ever greater simplicities which characterizes current policies. Nor can those who have devoted a lifetime to the study of education, of curriculum, of educational assessment match the amazing facility with which the intellectual giants who take on these responsibilities and those who rush to add their own twopennyworths to the debate stride from one simplification to another.

Thus major steps have been taken in this direction even as this book was being compiled.

At the time of going to press we must note several of these steps. First, it is clear that the emphasis of assessment in the early years is shifting from its previous focus on the whole of key stage 1 to a concern with attainment at the end of that stage, from a formative to a summative emphasis, therefore, and from teacher assessment to testing by Standard Assessment Tasks (SATs). Second, the development and the administration of any battery of SATs which attempts to address the more sophisticated aspects of educational achievement (as some of the SATs which have been developed seek to do), or even of achievement within the attainment targets, and to do so with some hope of producing results which are reasonably fair and informative, is proving cumbersome and, above all, expensive. (And the fact that this seems to have come as a surprise to all but those within education, who have been prophesying this for some time, is perhaps the greatest indictment of the amateur nature of current planning.) As a result the current Secretary of State – at time of going to press – has decreed, as the 1988 Act empowers him to do, that all such tests must now be (to quote from SEAC's own account of this decree) 'simple, rigorous, objective, manageable for both teachers and pupils, not disruptive of teaching programmes, time limited and capable of being administered to pupils simultaneously' (it being unclear whether this last requirement implies that all pupils should be able to do the tests at the same time or that the pupils should be able to do all the tests at the same time). Again one notes the simple faith of the ignorant – or the devious strategies and rhetoric of the clever. For we have seen that even the most sophisticated of test instruments can hope to offer only a limited level of validity and objectivity, so that for a Secretary of State for education to decree that tests must be produced which are time limited, simple and objective (to mention only three of the criteria listed) is analogous to a Minister of Health decreeing that medical researchers must produce an immediate, simple and effective cure for cancer. Indeed, the latter, although displaying comparable levels of megalomania, would be more credible, since the possibility of the ultimate discovery of a cure for cancer is far more realistic than the notion that we can invent some form of test which will satisfy all the criteria listed above.

We must also note that it is becoming increasingly clear – again as all those with any kind of understanding of the realities of schools and educational practice have been prophesying for some time – what impact this testing programme is having on schools, on teachers and, above all, on pupils. At the time of going to press, infant schools and departments are obsessed, in every sense of that term, with the practicalities of testing. It is a major disruption to the school as a whole; it is taking up all of the time of teachers of classes of top infants, and others too, as they administer the tests and record the results; teachers are complaining that they are SATed, SATurated but far from SATisfied by what they are currently being required to do; and it is looming far larger than anything of this kind ever should in the lives and minds of the six and seven-year-olds who are being tested. The ideal, expressed by the TGAT Report (DES, 1988a) that they should be tested as part of their normal classroom work and in such a way that they would not even be aware it was happening has proved to be the wishful thinking most teachers of young children knew it would be. Their anxieties and concerns are already beginning to show; and no one who has any understanding of education or sensitivity to young children's needs can possibly justify the model of education which this process is offering to young children at a most formative time in their development.

Furthermore, as these six- and seven-year-olds are being tested day-in-day-out in science, mathematics and English, four at a time, their colleagues, who are at any moment not being put through the tests are equally not receiving an education. They are being left to get on unaided and unsupported with pre-set work to enable their teachers to devote all their time to the testing process and to concentrate on whichever four pupils happen to be on the spot or in the hot seat at any given time. It is a travesty of anything one could call education at any age or stage. It is particularly reprehensible in the early years, when attitudes to learning and models of learning are still being established. And it makes Mr Gradgrind's lesson, as portrayed by, and indeed caricatured by, Charles Dickens in *Hard Times*, look positively progressive and imaginative.

It is not possible to predict what future inanities will emerge. It is possible, however, to identify the direction in which these policies are progressively trending. That trend is away from any complex notions of education as human development, notions which have been steadily rubbished as the products of woolly-minded idealists, who, in spite of the fact that most of them are in more direct contact with children, classrooms and schools than their critics, are dismissed as being out of touch with reality. Such notions are to be replaced by the simple, 'down-do-earth', hard-nosed, commercially oriented view of education as a simple matter of getting on (or not getting on), of competing and winning (of failing) and of demonstrating that you can jump through whatever hoops, or clear whatever hurdles, educational progress is deemed to consist of. For, whatever the rhetoric in which current policies are concealed, this is their true face.

It would be reassuring if one could believe that this reflected a different view or philosophy of education. For then it would be open to debate. And one of the attributes of those woolly-minded idealists who seek to promote a more sophisticated form of education is that they do so because they value debate, challenge, disagreement and the idea that other people may have a different point of view. The sad fact is, however, that current policies reflect nothing more than the absence of any view or philosophy, and the intention, as we saw above, of turning education into something else, a form of commercial transaction into which society need put no more, and preferably less, than it gets out.

There are important differences between these two approaches to educational provision – especially in the early years. And those differences have important implications not only for educational practice, or even for educational assessment, but for the very nature of the society in which we live and the direction in which that society itself is moving, or being led.

Educational assessment is a highly subtle matter, as we hope this book has shown. It has crucial implications for the quality of educational provision, as we hope we have also shown. Perhaps more important than either of these conclusions, however, is that the two together have a fundamental bearing on the kind of society we want or the kind of society which is created for us.

BIBLIOGRAPHY

Abbs, P. (1990) Market mania, *The Times Educational Supplement*, 14 September.

Ahlberg, J. and Ahlberg, A. (1978) *Each, Peach, Pear, Plum*, Kestrel/Penguin, Harmondsworth.

Aldrich, R. (1988) The National Curriculum: an historical perspective, in Lawton and Chitty (eds.) *op. cit.*, pp. 34–48.

Alexander, R. J. (1988) The National Curriculum and the languages of primary education. Unpublished paper given at the Primary Education Study Group's conference, Newby Bridge, 17–19 November.

Alexander, R. J. (1990) The training of primary teachers. Unpublished paper given at the NAPTEC Annual Conference, Birmingham, 11–12 May.

Alexander, R. J. (1984) *Primary Teaching*, Holt, Rinehart & Winston, London.

Allen, D. (1989) *English, Whose English?* NATE, London.

Allen, W. F., Ware, C. P. and Garrison, L. McK. (1867) *Slave Songs of the United States*.

Arnberg, L. (1987) *Raising Children Bilingually: The Pre-School Years*, Multilingual Matters, Avon, Clevedon.

Association for Science Education (1990) *Teacher Assessment: Making it Work for the Primary School*, ASE, Hatfield, Herts.

Athey, C. (1990) *Extending Thought in Young Children*, Paul Chapman, London.

Bain, B. and Yu, A. (1978) Toward an integration of Piaget and Vygotsky: a cross-cultural replication (France, Germany, Canada) concerning cognitive consequences of bilinguality, in M. Paradis (ed.) *Aspects of Bilingualism*, Hornbeam Press, Columbia, S. Carolina.

Bain, B. and Yu, A. (1980) Cognitive consequences of raising children bilingually: one parent, one language, *Canadian Journal of Psychology*, 34, pp. 304–13.

Baker, C. (1988) *Key Issues in Bilingualism and Bilingual Children*, Multilingual Matters, Clevedon, Avon.

Barnes, D. (1976) *From Communication to Curriculum*, Penguin, London.

Barrett, G. (ed.) (1989) *Disaffection from School? The Early Years*, Falmer, Lewes.

Barrs, M. (1990) *Words NOT Numbers: Assessment in English*, NAAE/NATE, London.

Barrs, M., Ellis, S., Hester, H. and Thomas, A. (1988) *The Primary Language Record Handbook*, ILEA/CLPE, London.

Barrs, M., Ellis, S., Hester, H. and Thomas, A. (1990) *Patterns of Learning. The Primary Language Record and the National Curriculum*, Centre for Language in Primary Education, London.

Bate, M. and Smith, M. (1978) *Manual for Assessment in Nursery Education*, NFER Publishing Company, Windsor.

Ben-Zeev, S. (1977) The influence of bilingualism on cognitive strategy and cognitive development, *Child Development,* Vol. 48, pp. 1009–18.

Bennett, N. and Kell, S. (1989) *A Good Start? Four Year Olds in Infant Schools,* Blackwell, Oxford.

Bialystok, E. (1987) Words as things. Development of word concept by bilingual children, *Studies in Second Language Acquisition,* Vol. 9, pp. 133–40.

Blenkin, G. M. (1988) Education and development: some implications for the curriculum in the early years, pp. 45–67 in Blyth (ed.) (1988) *op. cit.*

Blenkin, G. M. and Kelly, A. V. (1987) *The Primary Curriculum: A Process Approach to Curriculum Planning,* Harper & Row, London.

Blenkin, G. M. and Kelly, A. V. (eds.) (1988) *Early Childhood Education: A Developmental Curriculum,* Paul Chapman, London.

Blyth, A. (ed.) (1988) *Informal Primary Education Today: Essays and Studies,* Falmer, London.

Brice Heath, S. (1983) *Ways with Words. Language Life and Work in Communities and Classrooms,* Cambridge University Press, Cambridge.

Britton, J. (1987) Vygotsky's contribution to pedagogical theory, *English in Education,* Vol. 21, no. 33, pp. 22–6.

Broadfoot, P. M. (1979) *Assessment, Schools and Society,* Methuen, London.

Broadfoot, P. M. (1986) Alternatives to Public Examinations, in D. Nuttall (ed.) *op. cit.* (1986).

Browne, N. and France, P. (eds.) (1986) *Untying the Apron Strings,* Open University Press, Milton Keynes.

Bruce, T. (1987) *Early Childhood Education,* Hodder & Stoughton, London.

Bruner, J. S. (1980) *Under Five in Britain,* Grant McIntyre, London.

Bruner, J. S. (1983) *Child's Talk: Learning to Use Language,* Oxford University Press.

Bruner, J. S. (1986) *Actual Minds, Possible Worlds,* Harvard University Press, Cambridge, Mass.

Bruner, J. S. and Haste, H. (eds.) (1987) *Making Sense. The Child's Construction of the World,* Methuen, London.

Bryant, P. and Bradley, L. (1985) *Children's Reading Problems,* Blackwell, Oxford.

Carr, M. and Claxton, G. (1989) The costs of calculation, *New Zealand Journal of Educational Studies,* Vol. 24, no. 2, pp. 129–39.

Cazden, C. (1984) Play with language and metalinguistic awareness: one dimension of language experience, in M. Donaldson, R. Grieve and C. Pratt (eds.) *Early Childhood Development and Education,* Blackwell, Oxford.

Centre for Language in Primary Education/Inner London Education Authority (1988) *The Primary Language Record. Handbook for Teachers,* CLPE, London.

Centre for Language in Primary Education (1990a) *The Primary Learning Record,* CLPE, London.

Centre for Language in Primary Education (1990b) *Patterns of Learning,* CLPE, London.

Christian, C. C. (1976) Social and psychological implications of bilingual literacy, in A. Simoes Jnr. (ed.) *The Bilingual Child,* Academic Press, New York.

Clark, M. M. (1979) *Young Fluent Readers,* Heinemann, London.

Clay, M. M. (1979) *The Early Detection of Reading Difficulties*, Heinemann, Auckland, New Zealand.

Clift, P., Weiner, G. and Wilson, E. (1981) *Record Keeping in Primary Schools*, Schools Council Research Studies, Macmillan Educational, London.

Cole, M. (1975) Culture, cognition and IQ testing, *National Elementary Principal*, Vol. 54, pp. 49–52.

Cousins, J. (1990) 'Are your little Humpty Dumpties floating or sinking?' What sense do children of four make of the reception class at school? Different concepts at that time of transition, *Early Years*, Vol. 10, no. 2, pp. 28–38.

Crossland, H. (1990) Baseline assessment in language: a book-centred approach, *English in Education*, Vol. 24, no. 2, pp. 40–52.

Cummins, J. (1978a) Immersion programs: the Irish experience, *International Review of Education*, no. 24, pp. 273–82.

Cummins, J. (1978b) Educational implications of mother-tongue maintenance in minority language groups, *Canadian Modern Language Review*, no. 34, pp. 855–83.

Cummins, J. (1980) The cross-lingual dimensions of language proficiency: implications for bilingual education and the optimal age issue, *TESOL Quarterly*, no. 14(2), pp. 174–87.

Cummins, J. (1984) *Bilingualism and Special Education: Issues in Assessment and Pedagogy*, Multilingual Matters, Clevedon, Avon.

Curtis, S. J. (1948) *History of Education in Great Britain*, University Tutorial Press, London.

Curtis, S. J. and Boultwood, M. E. A. (1960) *An Introductory History of English Education since 1800*, University Tutorial Press, London.

Desforges, C. W. (ed.) (1989) *Early Childhood Education*, The British Journal of Educational Psychology Monograph Series No. 4, Scottish Academic Press, Edinburgh.

Diana v. California State Board of Education (1970) no. C–70 37 Rfp, US District Court of Northern California.

Donaldson, M. (1978) *Children's Minds*, Fontana, Glasgow.

Drummond, M. J. (1989) Early years education: contemporary challenges 1–15, in C. W. Desforges (ed.) *op. cit.*

Drummond, M. J., Lally, M. and Pugh, G. (1989) *Working with Children: Developing a Curriculum for the Early Years*, NCB/Nottingham Educational Supplies, Nottingham.

Early Years Curriculum Group (1989) *Early Childhood Education: The Early Years Curriculum and the National Curriculum*, Trentham Books, Stoke-on-Trent.

Edwards, A. D. (1976) *Language in Culture and Class*, Heinemann, Portsmouth.

Egan, K. (1988) *Primary Understanding: Education in Early Childhood*, Routledge, London.

Eisner, E. W. (1982) *Cognition and Curriculum: A Basis for Deciding What to Teach*, Longman, New York and London.

Eisner, E. (1985) *The Art of Educational Evaluation: A Personal View*, Falmer, Lewes.

Feldman, C. and Shen, M. (1971) Some language-related cognitive advantages of bilingual five year olds, *Journal of Genetic Psychology*, Vol. 118, pp. 235–44.

Feynman, R. P. (1988) *'What Do You Care What Other People Think?'* Unwin Hyman, London.

Fillmore, L. (1976) *The Second Time Around: Cognitive and Social Strategies in Second Language Acquisition*, Ph.D. Dissertation, Stanford University.

Fillmore, L. (1979) Individual differences in second language acquisition, in C. J. Fillmore, D. Kempler and W. S–Y Wang (eds.) *Individual Differences in Language Ability and Language Behaviour*, Academic Press, New York.

Fillmore, L. (1983) The language learner as an individual. Implications of research on individual differences for the ESL teacher, in M. A. Clarke and J. Handscombe (eds.) *On TESOL '82 Pacific Perspectives on Language Learning and Teaching*, TESOL, Washington DC.

Genesee, F., Tucker, G. R. and Lambert, W. E. (1978) The development of ethnic identity and ethnic role taking skills in children from different school settings, *International Journal of Psychology*, Vol. 13, pp. 39–57.

Ghaye, A. and Pascal, C. (1988) *Four Year Old Children in Reception Classrooms: Participant Perceptions and Practice*, Worcester College of Higher Education.

Gipps, C. (1988) What exams would mean for primary education, in Lawton and Chitty (eds.) *op. cit.*

Gipps, C., Steadman, S., Blackstone, T. and Stierer, B. (1983) *Testing Children: Standardized Testing in Local Education Authorities and Schools*, Heinemann, London.

Goddard, H. H. (1917) Mental tests and the immigrant, *Journal of Delinquency*, no. 2, p. 271.

Goodman, K. (ed.) (1973) *Miscue Analysis: Applications to Reading Instruction*, Urbana, ERIC/NCTE, USA.

Goodman, K. S. (1973) Psycholinguistics universals in the reading process, in F. Smith (ed.) *Psycholinguistics and Reading*, Holt, Rinehart & Winston, New York.

Grieve, R., Tunmer, W. E. and Pratt, C. (1984) Language awareness in children, in M. Donaldson, R. Grieve and C. Pratt (eds.) *Early Childhood Development and Education*, Blackwell, Oxford.

Guthrie, L. F. and Hall, W. S. (1983) Continuity/discontinuity in the function and use of language, in E. Gordon (ed.) *Review of Research in Education*, Vol. 10, F. E. Peacock, Itasca, Illinois.

Hakuta, K. (1986) *Mirror of Language. The Debate on Bilingualism*, Basic Books, New York.

Hannon, P., Long, R., Weinberger, J. and Whitehurst, L. (1985) *Involving Parents in the Teaching of Reading: Some Key Sources*, University of Sheffield.

Hargreaves, A. (1989) *Curriculum and Assessment Reform*, Open University Press, Milton Keynes.

Harrison, F. (1985) *A Father's Diary*, Fontana-Flamingo, London.

Harste, J. C., Woodward, V. A. and Burke, C. L. (1984) *Language Stories and Literacy Lessons*, Heinemann, Portsmouth, New Hampshire.

Hatch, E., Peck, S. and Wagner-Gough, J. (1979) A look at process in child second language acquisition, in E. Ochs and B. Schieffelin (eds.) *Developmental Pragmatics*, Academic Press, New York.

Hazareesingh, S., Simms, K. and Anderson, P. (1989) *Educating the Whole Child. A Holistic Approach to Education in Early Years*, Building Blocks, London.

Heath, S. R. (1983) *Ways with Words. Language, Life, and Work in Communities and Classrooms*, Cambridge University Press, Cambridge.

Holdaway, D. (1979) *The Foundations of Literacy*, Ashton Scholastic, Sydney.

Holmes, G. (1977) *The Idiot Teacher*, Spokesman, Nottingham.

Houlton, D. (1986) *Cultural Diversity in the Primary School*, Batsford, London.

Hughes, M. (1986) *Children and Number*, Blackwell, Oxford.

Hurst, V. (1991) *Planning for Early Learning: Education in the Years before Five*, Paul Chapman, London.

Ianco-Worrall, A. (1972) Bilingualism and cognitive development, *Child Development*, no. 43, pp. 1390–400.

Inner London Education Authority (1984) *Mealtime with Lily* (Phototalk Series), ILEA/Learning Resources Branch, London.

Inner London Education Authority (1985) *Improving Primary Schools* (The Thomas Report).

Isaacs, S. (1930) *Intellectual Growth in Young Children*, Routledge & Kegan Paul, London.

Isaacs, S. (1933) *Social Development in Young Children: A Study of Beginnings*, Routledge & Kegan Paul, London.

John-Steiner, V. (1985) The road to competence in an alien land: a Vygotskian perspective on bilingualism, in J. V. Wertsch (ed.) *Culture, Communication and Cognition, Vygotskian Perspectives*, Cambridge University Press.

Johnson, J. E. (1988) Psychological theory and early education, in Pellegrini (ed.) *op. cit.* pp. 1–21.

Jones, K. (1989) *Right Turn*, Hutchinson, Radius, London.

Kaufman, A. S. (1979) *Intelligent Testing with the WISC–R*, Wiley, New York.

Kelly, A. V. (1990) *The National Curriculum: A Critical Review*, Paul Chapman, London.

Kimberley, K. (1990) The third limb. Assessment and the National Curriculum, *The English Magazine*, Vol. 23, Summer, pp. 19–26.

King, R. (1978) *All Things Bright and Beautiful? A Sociological Study of Infants' Classrooms*, Wiley, Chichester.

Krashen, S. D. (1981) *Principles and Practice in Second Language Acquisition*, Pergamon Press, Oxford.

Lally, M. (1991) *The Nursery Teacher in Action*, Paul Chapman, London.

Lambert, W. E. (1977) The effect of bilingualism on the individual: cognitive and sociocultural, in P. A. Hornby, (ed.) *Bilingualism: Psychological, Social and Educational Implications*, Academic Press, New York.

Lambert, W. E. and Tucker, G. R. (1972) *Bilingual Education of Children: The St. Lambert Experiment*, Newbury House, Rowley, Mass.

Lawton, D. and Chitty, C. (eds.) (1988) *The National Curriculum*, Bedford Way Paper 33, Institute of Education, London.

Lawton, D. (ed.) (1989) *The Education Reform Act: Choice and Control*, Hodder, London.

Liedtke, W. W. and Nelson, L. D. (1968) Concept formation and bilingualism, *Alberta Journal of Education Research*, Vol. 14, pp. 225–32.

McDermott, R. P. (1978) Relating and learning: an analysis of two classroom reading groups, in R. Snuy (ed.) *Linguistics and Reading*, Newbury House, Rowley, Mass.

Marcus, U. C., Feldman, D. H. and Gardner, H. (1988) Dimensions of mind in early childhood, in Pellegrini (ed.) *op. cit.*, pp. 25–38.

Marland, M. (1987) *Multilingual Britain*, CILTR, London.

Meek, M. (1982) *Learning to Read*, Bodley Head, London.

Meek, M. (1991) *On Being Literate*, Bodley Head, London.

Merttens, R. and Vass, J. (1990a) Assessing the National Curriculum: blueprints without tools, in *Primary Teaching Studies*, Vol. 5, no. 3, June 1990, pp. 222–39.

Merttens, R. and Vass, J. (1990b) *IMPACT – Sharing Maths Culture*, Falmer Press, Lewes.

Metz, M. (1988) The development of mathematical understanding, in Blenkin and Kelly (eds.) (1988) *op. cit.*, pp. 184–201.

Michaels, S. (1986) Narrative presentations: an oral preparation for literacy with 1st graders, in J. Cook-Gumperz (ed.) *The Social Construction of Literacy*, Cambridge University Press.

Mohatt, G. and Erickson, F. (1981) Cultural differences in teaching styles in an Odawa school: a sociolinguistic approach, in H. T. Trueba, G. P. Guthrie and K. H. Au (eds.) *Culture and the Bilingual Classroom: Studies in Classroom Ethnography*, Newbury House, Rowley, Mass.

Montessori, M. (1912) *The Montessori Method*, Heinemann, London.

Murphy, R. and Torrance, H. (1988) *The Changing Face of Educational Assessment*, Open University Press, Milton Keynes.

National Union of Teachers (1990) *A Strategy for the Curriculum*, Hamilton House, London.

Nuttall, D. (1989) National assessment: complacency or misinterpretation? in Lawton (ed.) *op. cit.*

Nuttall, D. L. (ed.) (1986) *Assessing Educational Achievement*, Falmer, London and Philadelphia.

Nuttall, D. L. (1990) Unpublished discussion paper on National Curriculum Assessment, Bera Policy Task Group on Assessment.

O'Neill, E. (1977) see, Holmes, G.

Pascal, C. (1990) *Under-Fives in the Infant Classroom*, Trentham Books, Stoke-on-Trent.

Peal, E. and Lambert, W. E. (1962) The relation of bilingualism and intelligence, *Psychological Monographs: General and Applied*, 76, 546, pp. 1–23.

Pellegrini, A. D. (ed.) (1988) *Psychological Bases for Early Education*, Wiley, New York.

Perera, K. (1988) Understanding language, in N. Mercer (ed.) *Language and Literacy from an Educational Perspective*, Vol. 2, Open University Press, Milton Keynes.

Phillips, S. (1972) Participant structures and communicative competence: Warm Springs children in community and classroom, in C. Cazden, D. Hymes and V. J. John (eds.) *Functions of Language in the Classroom*, Teachers' College Press, New York.

Pollard, A. (1990) Assessment at seven: a new research project, *The Redland Papers*. An occasional publication of the Faculty of Education, Bristol Polytechnic. Summer 1990, pp. 20–2.
Pollard, A. and Tann, S. (1987) *Reflective Teaching in the Primary School*, Cassell, London.
Reid, J. (1983) Into print: reading and language growth, in M. Donaldson, R. Grieve and C. Pratt (eds.) *Early Childhood Development and Education*, Blackwell, Oxford.
Ribeiro, J. L. (1980) Testing Portuguese immigrant children: cultural patterns and group differences in responses to the WISC-R, in D. P. Macedo (ed.) *Issues in Portuguese Bilingual Education*, National Assessment and Dissemination Center for Bilingual Education, Cambridge, Mass.
Richards, R. (1972) *Early Experiences. Schools Council 5/13 Project*, Macdonald Educational for the Schools Council, London.
Richards, R. (1988) Learning through science in the early years, in Blenkin and Kelly (eds.), (1988) *op. cit.*, pp. 218–30.
Rogers, C. (1989) Early admission: early labelling, in C. W. Desforges (ed.) *op. cit.*, pp. 94–107.
Salmon, P. (ed.) (1980) *Coming to Know*, Routledge & Kegan Paul, London.
Sapir, E. (1970) *Culture, Language and Personality*, University of California Press, Berkeley.
Schilling, M., Hargreaves, L., Harlen, W., with Russell, T. (1990) *Written Tasks, Assessing Science in the Primary Classroom*, Paul Chapman, London.
Simon, B. (1985) *Does Education Matter?* Lawrence & Wishart, London.
Skutnabb-Kangas, T. (1984) *Bilingualism or Not – The Education of Minorities*, Multilingual Matters Ltd, Clevedon, Avon.
Smith, F. (1985) *Reading* (2nd edn), Cambridge University Press.
Smith, P. K. (1988) Children's play and its role in early development: a re-evaluation of the 'play ethos', in Pellegrini (ed.) *op. cit.*, pp. 207–26.
Stenhouse, L. (1975) *An Introduction to Curriculum Research and Development*, Heinemann, London.
Stenhouse, L. (ed.) (1980) *Curriculum Research and Development in Action*, Heinemann, London.
Stevenson, C. (1988) *Focus on 4*, Cambridgeshire County Council.
Swain, M. and Cummins, J. (1979) Bilingualism, cognitive functioning and education, *Language Teaching and Linguistics Abstracts*, Vol. 12, no. 1, pp. 4–18.
Tizard, B., Blatchford, P., Burke, J., Farquhar, C. and Plewis, I. (1988) *Young Children at School in the Inner City*, Lawrence Erlbaum Associates, Hove.
Tizard, B. and Hughes, M. (1984) *Young Children Learning*, Fontana, London.
Torrance, H. (1989) Theory, practice and politics in the development of assessment, *Cambridge Journal of Education*, Vol. 19, no. 2, pp. 183–90.
Tyler, R. W. (1949) *Basic Principles of Curriculum and Instruction*, University of Chicago Press.
Tyler, S. (1979) *Keele Pre-School Assessment Guide*, NFER/Nelson, Windsor.
Tyler, S. (1980) *Keele Pre-School Assessment Guide (Experimental Edition)*, NFER Publishing Company, Windsor.
Vygotsky, L. S. (1962) *Thought and Language*, MIT Press, Cambridge, Mass.

Vygotsky, L. S. (1978) *Mind in Society. The Development of Higher Psychological Processes*, Harvard University Press, Cambridge, Mass.

Vygotsky, L. S. (1986) *Thought and Language* (revised and edited by A. Kozulin), MIT Press, Cambridge, Mass.

Wade, B. (ed.) (1990) *Reading for Real*, Open University Press, Milton Keynes.

Walden, R. and Walkerdine, V. (1982) *Guts and Mathematics: The Early Years*, Bedford Way Papers no. 8, Institute of Education, London.

Waterland, L. (1990) Statutory reading, *Books for Keeps*, Vol. 63, July, pp. 4–5.

Wells, G. (1985) *Language, Learning and Education*, NFER/Nelson, Windsor.

Wells, G. (1986) *The Meaning Makers. Children Learning Language and Using Language to Learn*, Hodder & Stoughton, Sevenoaks.

Whitbread, N. (1972) *The Evolution of the Nursery-Infant School*, Routledge & Kegan Paul, London.

Whitehead, M. R. (1988) Testing . . . Testing . . . Can a broadly based early years curriculum survive the introduction of testing for seven year olds?, *Curriculum*, Vol. 9, no. 2, pp. 69–73.

Williams, R. (1975) The BITCH-100: a culture-specific test, *Journal of Afro-American Issues*, Vol. 3, pp. 103–16.

Wolf, D. P. (1988) Opening up assessment 24–29, *Educational Leadership*, December 1987/January 1988.

Wolfendale, S. (1989) Special needs in early education, in Desforges (ed.) *op. cit.*, pp. 110–27.

Wood, D., McMahon, L. and Cranstoun, Y. (1980) *Working with Under Fives*, Grant McIntyre, London.

Yard, L. (1990) Monitoring and assessing development, in B. Wade, *op. cit.*

OFFICIAL PUBLICATIONS REFERRED TO IN THE TEXT

Central Advisory Council for Education (1963) *Half Our Future* (The Newsom Report), HMSO, London.

Central Advisory Council for Education (1967) *Children and Their Primary Schools* (The Plowden Report), HMSO, London.

Department of Education and Science (1975) *A Language for Life* (The Bullock Report), HMSO, London.

Department of Education and Science (1978) *Special Educational Needs* (The Warnock Report), HMSO, London.

Department of Education and Science (1982) *Mathematics Counts* (The Cockcroft Report), HMSO, London.

Department of Education and Science (1984) *English from 5–16*, HMSO, London.

Department of Education and Science (1987a) *The National Curriculum 5–16: A Consultative Document*, HMSO, London.

Department of Education and Science/Assessment of Performance Unit (1987b) *Design and Technological Activity: A Framework for Assessment*, HMSO, London.

Department of Education and Science (1988a) *National Curriculum: Task Group on Assessment and Testing: A Report*, HMSO, London.

Department of Education and Science (1988b) *Report of the Committee of Inquiry into the Teaching of English Language* (The Kingman Report), HMSO, London.

Department of Education and Science (1988c) *English for Ages 5–11. Proposals of the Secretaries of State* (The Cox Report), NCC/HMSO, London.

Department of Education and Science (1988d) *The Education Reform Act. The School Curriculum and Assessment*, HMSO, London.

Department of Education and Science (1989a) *ERA: A Bulletin for School Teachers and Governors*, Issue 4, Autumn, HMSO, London.

Department of Education and Science (1989b) *National Curriculum: From Policy to Practice*, HMSO, London.

Department of Education and Science (1989c) *Aspects of Primary Education: The Education of Children Under Five*, HMSO, London.

Department of Education and Science (1990a) *English 5–16*, HMSO, London.

Department of Education and Science (1990b) *Starting with Quality* (The Rumbold Report), HMSO, London.

Education, Science and Arts Committee (1989) *Educational Provision for the Under Fives*, HMSO, London.

Home Affairs Committee (1986–87) *Bangladeshis in Britain*, Vol. 1, HMSO, London.

Report of the Schools Inquiry Commission (The Taunton Report) (1868).

School Examinations and Assessment Council (1990a) *Children's Work Assessed*, HMSO, London.

School Examinations and Assessment Council (1990b) *A Guide to Teacher Assessment, A Source Book of Teacher Assessment*, HMSO, London.

School Examinations and Assessment Council (1991) *Records of Achievement in Primary Schools*, HMSO, London.

School Examination and Assessment Council, Evaluation and Monitoring Unit (1991) *The Assessment of Performance in Design and Technology*, HMSO, London.

Secondary Schools Examinations Council (1960) *Secondary School Examinations other than the GCE* (The Beloe Report), HMSO, London.

INDEX OF NAMES

INDEX OF SUBJECTS

Printed in the United Kingdom
by Lightning Source UK Ltd.
110828UKS00001B/106-117